The 1996 McGraw-Hill Training and Performance Sourcebook

Mel Silberman

Assisted by
Carol Auerbach

D1716127

McGraw-Hill

New York San Francisco Washington, D.C. Auckland Bogotá
Caracas Lisbon London Madrid Mexico City Milan
Montreal New Delhi San Juan Singapore
Sydney Tokyo Toronto

International Standard Serial Number:
The 1996 McGraw-Hill Training and Performance Sourcebook
ISSN 1084-1342

1 2 3 4 5 6 7 8 9 0   EDW/EDW   9 0 0 9 8 7 6 5   (Paperback)
1 2 3 4 5 6 7 8 9 0   EDW/EDW   9 0 0 9 8 7 6 5   (Looseleaf)

ISBN 0-07-057653-X (Paperback)
ISBN 0-07-057654-8 (Looseleaf)

The sponsoring editor for this book was Richard Narramore, the editing supervisor was Fred Dahl, the designer was Inkwell Publishing Services, and the production supervisor was Pamela Pelton.

Printed and bound by Edwards Brothers.

McGraw-Hill books are available at special quantity discounts to use as premiums and sales promotions, or for use in corporate training programs. For more information, please write to the Director of Special Sales, McGraw-Hill, 11 West 19th Street, New York, NY 10011. Or contact your local bookstore.

Are you interested in being a contributor to *The 1997 McGraw-Hill Training and Performance Sourcebook?*

In the course of your professional work, you have probably developed exercises, handouts, instruments, short articles, and other printed materials that could be useful to a wide audience of consultants, trainers, and team leaders. Consider your favorite piece of work for publication. The *1997 Sourcebook* will contain another 40 practical tools to improve learning and performance. Would you like to contribute one of them?

For more information, contact:

Mel Silberman, Editor
The McGraw-Hill Training and Performance Sourcebook
c/o Active Training
26 Linden Lane
Princeton, NJ 08540
609-924-8157
609-924-4250 fax
mel@tigger.jvnc.net

CONTENTS

TOPICAL INDEX
Find a Tool for Your Specific Topic

In the place of a traditional index is the following classification by topic of the 40 tools found in *The 1996 McGraw-Hill Training and Performance Sourcebook.*

PREFACE

Welcome to the inaugural edition of *The McGraw-Hill Training and Performance Sourcebook,* a yearly collection of practical tools to develop human resources.

Along with its companion, *The McGraw-Hill Team and Organization Development Sourcebook, The McGraw-Hill Training and Performance Sourcebook* provides the latest cutting-edge advice and learning aids on topics important to today's public and private sector organizations. While *The Team and Organization Development Sourcebook* emphasizes systemwide issues, *The McGraw-Hill Training and Performance Sourcebook* focuses on development and support at the individual level of the organization.

The McGraw-Hill Training and Performance Sourcebook includes discussion of both training and nontraining solutions to performance problems. You will find several materials, prepared by leading experts, that enhance your efforts as a trainer, instructor, or coach. You will also discover ways to support individual performance through such means as mentoring and performance technology.

The 1996 Sourcebook contains 40 training activities, assessment instruments, handouts, and practical guides—creating a ready-to-use toolkit for trainers, HRD consultants, performance support specialists, and subject matter experts. It is also invaluable for managers and other organizational representatives who are interested in coaching, training, learning, and performance development. Best of all, because these tools are reproducible, they can be shared with others.

Here are some of the topics covered in *The 1996 McGraw-Hill Training and Performance Sourcebook:*

✓ Alternatives to classroom training

✓ Career development

✓ Communication skills

✓ Computer training

✓ Diversity and cross-cultural awareness

✓ Issues in the workplace

✓ Learning and training techniques

✓ Management development

- ✓ Performance support
- ✓ Personal effectiveness
- ✓ Sales
- ✓ Training design

I hope you will find *The 1996 McGraw-Hill Training and Performance Sourcebook* to be a one-stop resource you can draw on again and again in your efforts to facilitate learning and support performance improvement.

Mel Silberman
Princeton, New Jersey

TRAINING ACTIVITIES

In this section of *The 1996 McGraw-Hill Training and Performance Sourcebook,* you will find 14 training activities. They are designed to:

✓ Introduce training topics.

✓ Practice skills.

✓ Promote attitude changes.

✓ Increase knowledge.

✓ Stimulate discussion.

✓ Foster participation and retention.

✓ Enhance concepts.

You can use these activities in a variety of settings:

✓ Classroom-based training sessions

✓ Meetings and retreats

✓ One-to-one coaching

✓ Distance learning

✓ Consultations

All the actitivies featured here are highly participatory. They are designed with the belief that learning and change occur best through *experience* and *reflection.* As opposed to preaching or lecturing, experiential activities place people directly in a concrete situation. Typically, participants are asked to solve a problem, complete an assignment, or communicate information. Often, the task can be quite challenging. Sometimes, it can also be a great deal of fun. The bottom line, however, is that participants become active partners in the learning of new concepts or in the development of new ideas.

The experiences contained in the activities you are about to read can also be of two kinds: *simulated* and *real-world.* Although some may find them to be artificial, well designed simulations can provide an effective analogy to real-world experiences. They also have the advantage of being time-saving shortcuts to longer, drawn-out activities. Sometimes, of course, there is no substitute for real-world experience. Activities that engage teams in actual, ongoing work can serve as a powerful mechanism for change.

Experience, by itself, is not always "the best teacher." Reflecting on the experience, however, can yield wisdom and insight. You will find that the training activities in this section contain helpful guidelines for reflection. Expect a generous selection of questions to process or debrief the actual activities.

All the activities here have been written for ease of use. A concise overview of each activity is provided. You will be guided, step by step, through the activity instructions. All the necessary participant materials are included. For your photocopying convenience, these materials are on separate pages. Any materials you need to prepare in advance have been kept to a minimum. Special equipment or physical arrangements are seldom needed.

Best of all, the activities are designed so that you can easily modify or customize them to your specific requirements. Also, time allocations are readily adaptable. Furthermore, many of the activities are "frame exercises"—generic activities that can be used for many topics or subject areas. You will find it easy to plug in the content relevant to your group's circumstances.

As you conduct any of these activities, bear in mind that experiential activity is especially successful if you do a good job as facilitator. Here are some common mistakes people make when facilitating experiential activities:

1. *Motivation:* Participants aren't invited to buy into the activity themselves or sold the benefits of joining in. Participants don't know what to expect during the exercise.

2. *Directions:* Instructions are lengthy and unclear. Participants cannot visualize what the facilitator expects from them.

3. *Group Process:* Subgroups are not composed effectively. Group formats are not changed to fit the requirements of each activity. Subgroups are left idle.

4. *Energy:* Activities move too slowly. Participants are sedentary. Activities are long or demanding when they need to be short or relaxed. Participants do not find the activity challenging.

5. *Processing:* Participants are confused and/or overwhelmed by the questions posed to them. There is a poor fit between the facilitator's questions and the goals of the activity. The facilitator shares his/her opinions before first hearing the participants' views.

To avoid these pitfalls, follow these steps:

I. Introduce the activity.

   1. Explain your objectives.
   2. Sell the benefits.
   3. Convey enthusiasm.
   4. Connect the activity to previous activities.
   5. Share personal feelings and express confidence in participants.

II. Help participants know what they are expected to do.
   1. Speak slowly.
   2. Use visual backup.
   3. Define important terms.
   4. Demonstrate the activity.

III. Manage the group process.
   1. Form groups in a variety of ways.
   2. Vary the number of people in any activity based upon that exercise's specific requirements.
   3. Divide participants into teams before giving further directions.
   4. Give instructions separately to groups in a multipart activity.
   5. Keep people busy.
   6. Inform the subgroups about time frames.

IV. Keep participants involved.
   1. Keep the activity moving.
   2. Challenge the participants.
   3. Reinforce participants for their involvement in the activity.
   4. Build physical movement into the activity.

V. Get participants to reflect on the activity's implications.
   1. Ask relevant questions.
   2. Carefully structure the first processing experiences.
   3. Observe how participants are reacting to the group processing.
   4. Assist a subgroup that is having trouble processing an activity.
   5. Hold your own reactions until after hearing from participants.

CULTURE MATES: A CROSS-CULTURAL SIMULATION

Jo Renee Fine

Jo Renee Fine, *Ph.D., directs the Training Center for Diversity and Quality Management, a division of Cicatelli Associates, Inc. (505 Eighth Avenue, New York, NY 10018, 212-594-7741), a private, nonprofit group that assists human service and health care agencies to strengthen their services through employee training and organizational development. She also is involved in numerous community activities, including serving as the New York chair for "Hands across the Campus," a prejudice-reduction program sponsored by the American Jewish Committee.*

Overview

Culture Mates is a highly interactive, nonthreatening, and enjoyable diversity exercise designed to (1) contribute to participants' understanding of how bonds develop among individuals who share the same cultural traditions, (2) heighten participants' awareness of the feelings experienced by members of cultural minority groups, and (3) help participants to identify commonplace, daily interactions that have a strong cultural basis.

To complete this exercise, each participant is assigned to one of seven hypothetical cultural groups and is given a description of the way members of that group greet one another. There must be at least two participants who have been given the same description; however, a culture may have more than two members. If the group is very large, it is recommended that 14 participants volunteer (2 per culture) to demonstrate the exercise for the full group.

Suggested Time

20–30 minutes

Materials Needed

Form A (Descriptions of Cultures A through G)
Note: Each culture should be placed on a separate sheet of paper or card.

Procedure

1. Before beginning the exercise, count and shuffle the number of culture descriptions that matches the number of participants who will take part in the exercise.

2. Tell participants that this exercise will give them an opportunity to experience what it feels like to be part of a culture that has traditions that are different from their own. In addition, they will be able to explore what can happen when different groups with different norms and traditions come together in the same setting.

3. Hand out one culture description, face down, to each participant. Stress that participants should not allow others to see the description on their sheets.

4. Give participants time to read their descriptions and then ask them to get up and search for the other member(s) of their culture. Indicate that they must identify their "mate(s)" by walking around the room and practicing their culture's traditional greeting behavior until they find one or more persons who display exactly the same behavior. Emphasize that no one should speak unless their greeting description has a verbal component.

5. Allow participants at least 5 minutes to find their mate(s). The time frame for this part of the exercise will depend on the number of people participating, with a larger group requiring more time. Instruct participants that, when they find their mate(s), they should remain standing but stay with the members of their culture. While they await the end of the exercise, ask them to discuss how they feel about the way in which members of their culture greet one another.

6. When time is up, stop the exercise even if not everyone has located his or her mate(s). One by one, ask each group to demonstrate to the others the particular greeting tradition for the assigned culture. If some participants have not yet found the other members of their culture, they should now be able to readily identify where they belong.

7. Processing of this exercise should focus on how participants felt during their search, what they experienced when they found their mate(s) or how they felt if they were not able to find other members of their culture. The exercise is most effective when participants are able to discuss their feelings about the experience, for example, feeling rejected or frustrated if they could not find their mate or happy and relieved when the contact was made. Discussion may be generalized to include participants' observations about why people tend to feel most comfortable with what is familiar and uncomfortable with others whose behavior is different and/or not readily understood. If appropriate to the overall content of the workshop, the group might also describe actual cultural differences in greeting traditions in various cultural groups, as well as other cultural differences that are manifested in daily human interaction.

If there are observers as well as participants in the exercise, ask observers to comment on what they noticed about individual interactions. For example, what behavior did they see? What facial expressions and body language were apparent?

8. Specific questions you might ask could include the following:

   ✓ How did you feel when you were able to locate the other member(s) of your culture?

   ✓ How did you feel if you were unable to locate your mate(s)?

   ✓ How did you feel if you realized that a person who approached you (or whom you approached) was not a member of your group?

   ✓ How do people sometimes relate to strangers who have different customs and traditions?

   ✓ If you were a member of a cultural group that prohibited physical contact, how did you feel if someone tried to touch you? What happens in real life to many people whose culture prohibits being touched by strangers?

   ✓ How did you feel if you reached out to touch another person's hand and he or she moved away from you? Does this ever happen in real life? What are the consequences?

   ✓ Do any elements of these fictional descriptions fit real cultures? Which elements? Which cultures?

   ✓ Have you ever been in a situation in which you felt uncomfortable because you were not sure what the cultural norms were? What did you do? Was there anyone you could ask?

   ✓ Have you ever been in a situation where someone had contact with your cultural group but did not know the norms for expected behavior, for example, at a wedding or a funeral? What did the person do? How did others respond?

   ✓ To what extent do we expect others to assimilate to our own cultural norms and traditions? To what extent are we willing to assimilate to the norms and traditions of others? Can we decline to assimilate and still have positive interactions with those who are different? How can this be achieved?

9. Conclude the exercise by pointing out that even a behavior as simple as a greeting is culturally determined. Note that lack of familiarity with the cultural norms and traditions of others can lead to a lack of communication and failure to establish credibility with others.

Variation You can be as creative with this exercise as you wish. For example, you might tell participants, "It is the year 2500 and you are representatives of seven different planets who are attending an interplanetary conference to discuss (name a topic that is relevant for participants). It is important that you identify the members of your group in order to vote on certain issues. However, everyone here looks exactly alike and the only way that you can find your culture mate(s) is to find conference participants who share your traditional custom for greeting others from the same culture. So, hurry up and see how quickly you can locate your culture mate(s).

DESCRIPTIONS OF CULTURES A THROUGH G FORM A

Culture A

In your culture, no one *ever* speaks or smiles when greeting another member of the group. Members approach one another silently and solemnly, bow and then turn their backs to one another.

Culture B

When greeting other members of your culture, no one *ever* speaks or smiles. Members approach one another without speaking or smiling and *never* look the other person in the eyes. Looking at another person directly in the eyes is considered highly insulting and you must avoid this behavior at all costs. Members of the culture always extend their *left* hand to shake hands with the other person.

Culture C

In your culture, no one speaks when greeting. However, eye contact is very important, and as members approach one another they *always* look the other person directly in the eyes and then shake hands with their *left* hands. If another person should avoid looking you in the eyes, speak to you, or try to shake your right hand, you should indicate, nonverbally, that his or her behavior is totally unacceptable.

Culture D

Members of your culture may greet one another any way they wish. However, they must *always* say the words "Hi Ho Hello" when they approach someone from the group.

8

Culture E

In your culture, no one speaks, smiles, or looks the other person in the eye when greeting. When members approach one another, they hold out their right hands to the other person and wait until the person either takes their hand or moves away.

Culture F

In your culture, members do not speak when greeting, but they *always* smile and laugh when they see one another and are generally very friendly, even to members of other cultures. It is important to remember, however, that your cultural norms strictly forbid *any* physical contact with another person. If someone from another culture tries to touch you, you must let them know (nonverbally) that you are offended and feel uncomfortable with their behavior.

Culture G

In your culture, members are very happy people and laugh as much as possible. They are extremely uncomfortable being around people who are not as happy as they are. To find out if someone else is a member of your group, you will have to approach the other person and laugh out loud. If the other person does not laugh in return, you will know that he or she does not belong to your culture. If the person does laugh in return, you should immediately make physical contact with the other person, for example, by hugging (if you are comfortable), shaking hands, or touching the other person on the shoulder.

UNLOCKING CREATIVITY: A PUZZLE GAME

2

Jeanne Baer

Jeanne Baer *is president of Creative Training Solutions (1649 South 21st Street, Lincoln, NE 68502, 800-410-3178, jbaer@grex.cyberspace.org). The company provides training, facilitation, and program design services to clients as diverse as Chrysler, Burlington Northern, IDS, the International Festivals Association, and the Travel Industry Association of America. She teaches at Southeast Community College, writes for* **Training Media Review,** *and is a past president of the Lincoln, Nebraska, chapter of the American Society for Training and Development.*

Overview This activity allows participants a chance to meet and work with new people and exchange their opinions about a facet of creativity before your session actually begins. Throughout the session, it helps participants stay "in the ball game" by reporting their opinions to the whole group. *Unlocking Creativity* will work with anywhere from 8 to 48 participants.

Suggested Time 45–60 minutes

Materials Needed ✓ Eight simple puzzles you have made, each featuring one of the discussed questions that comprise this training session.

✓ Form A: Eight Tips to Unlock Creativity

Procedure 1. Before the session, make your eight puzzles. Use 8½ by 11 inch sheets of paper in various colors. Each puzzle features one of the letters in the word "c–r–e–a–t–i–v–e" and explains one creativity tip based on a word beginning with that letter.

2. Once you have prepared each sheet, plan to hand them to participants as they arrive for the session. If you have only 8 participants, each will receive an intact sheet, uncut into puzzle pieces. If you have 16 participants, cut each sheet in half, mix them up, and hand a half a puzzle to each person as you greet them at the door. If you have 24 participants, cut each sheet in thirds, and so on.

   If you do not have multiples of 8 participants, some of your sheets will be cut into more sheets than others. If you have, say, 12 participants, you cut four of your sheets in half (and four pairs of people will solve these) and you keep the other four sheets intact.

At any rate, if you have cut some of the sheets into puzzle pieces, instruct people to find and sit with their "puzzlemates," and begin to consider the tip and question posed on their assembled puzzle. If you have shuffled the pieces well, people will not end up sitting with the same people that they walked in the door with.

Reinforce your directions by also having them posted on a transparency or flip chart welcome page.

3. Once everyone has arrived and is seated with their puzzlemates and it is time to begin, welcome and thank them for sitting with and getting to know new people. Remind them that one of the best ways to come up with innovative ideas is to brainstorm with new and different people.

4. Distribute Form A. Explain that it contains eight creativity tips. Ask each participant or group of participants to read the tip corresponding to the letter that they have obtained and discuss the question(s) listed below the tip. Give them 5 to 6 minutes to reflect on the questions posed on their puzzle and decide what they want to report to the larger group.

5. Next, call on the groups in order of the letters in "c–r–e–a–t–i–v–e" and facilitate the discussion. Although some questions may take more or less time to discuss, you'll have an average of about 5 minutes per question. If you have time, you may include any of your own learning points, or short exercises, as appropriate.

Variations 1. To encourage people to find their puzzlemates quickly, offer prizes for the members of the first group to fully assemble their puzzle.

2. Type your accompanying handouts with one sentence that summarizes each tip, but leave out one word of each sentence. This word *will* appear on the matching puzzles; so when you come to that tip or concept in your lecture, you can call on the group that has that puzzle, and they can "fill in the blank" for the whole group.

3. If you have a large group with little space to mill around in, avoid "puzzling" frustration by making the task easier. Be sure each puzzle is on a different colored stock and have a tent card of that colored stock on the tables where you would like the holders of that color to gather. Then direct the participants, as they arrive, to simply wander among the tables until they find the tent card that matches the color of their puzzle piece.

C: Ask *crazy* questions.

Often, those new to a job or a project ask questions that those with more experience consider dumb or crazy. Frequently, these questions lead to a real breakthrough by getting "out of the box." A few such questions are "Does anyone actually look at that report?" or "Why have we always done it that way?" or "How does this really work?"

What "crazy" questions would be good to ask in your organization, department, or personal life?

R: *Recognize* flashes of inspiration; then *Record* them!

Creative ideas often happen out of the blue. When do you have flashes of inspiration? In the shower or tub? When you are driving or jogging?

How can you be sure to capture these sudden ideas so that they don't get away?

E: *Exercise* before beginning a challenging mental task.

It's a good idea to limber up the mind before putting it to strenuous work.

Do you know of any mental warm-up exercises to use before a brainstorming session? Can you give an example of how you have taken the time to be wild and crazy and let in some creative thoughts?

A: *Adapt* other people's ideas for your own use.

If you are observant, you can pick up great ideas any-where—the dry cleaners, a fast-food restaurant, a bank, from a friend or a competitor!

Can you think of any times when you noticed a product, service or idea used by someone else and then were able to adapt it? (The idea need not be a big one to be valuable!)

T: *Try* new methods to generate ideas.

Have you tried mind mapping? Have you ever solved a problem by finding a metaphor for your problem? Or have you magnified, minified, rearranged, reversed, combined, substituted, or modified ideas to generate new ones?

What are some ways to come up with new ideas when your own idea well has run dry?

I: *Invent* little ideas, not just big ones.

If people believe the myth that the only truly creative ideas are flashy breakthroughs, they will overlook some terrific small ideas that add up to large improvement, or they give up trying to be creative.

What are some examples of small but effective ideas (in any environment—home, work, and the like) that you or someone else has come up with lately? How are such ideas recognized?

V: *Vary* your *Viewpoint.*

Some ways to vary your viewpoint are to take a new route to work, browse through different magazines than you usually would, or try new hobbies.

Have you tried any of these viewpoint changers? What others can you suggest?

E: *Eliminate* your fear of failure.

Think of a time when you learned from a mistake or failure. Can you see how experimenting, risking, and failing can result in greater creativity?

How can you be sure you look at mistakes in a positive way?

IS IT OR ISN'T IT? CASE STUDIES IN SEXUAL HARASSMENT

Karen Cherwony

Karen Cherwony, *Ed.D., is director, Human Resource Development, at Temple University (Personal Services, 204A U.S.B., 1601 North Broad Street, Philadelphia, PA 19122, 215-204-1669). She is responsible for a variety of training and organizational development programs at the university and its hospital, including sexual harassment awareness training. Karen is an adjunct professor of social administration at Temple University and has consulted with a variety of governmental, educational, and corporate clients.*

Overview   Sexual harassment is a serious workplace issue that is defined by federal laws and regulations and often specific organizational policies. Much confusion and disagreement still exist, however, over what behaviors fall within the definitions of quid pro quo and hostile work environment sexual harassment. The case studies used in this design are intended to clarify the types of behaviors that are considered sexual harassment. In addition, this design also encourages participants to reveal their perceptions of what is and what is not harassment. Discussion questions center on appropriate actions that should be taken to prevent and respond to sexual harassment complaints.

Suggested Time   60 minutes

Materials Needed   ✓ Form A (What Is Sexual Harassment?)
✓ Form B (Sexual Harassment Case Studies)

Procedure   1. Distribute Form A to participants. Ask them to read the definitions and offer to provide any clarification.

2. Divide participants into groups of no more than seven members.

3. Assign each group a case study. If there are enough participants to form more than five groups, you can assign two groups the same case. Ask each group to select someone to report on the group's discussion. Allow the groups 15 minutes to discuss the cases.

4. Supplement the reports by each group with information that
   - ✓ Defines quid pro quo and hostile work environment sexual harassment
   - ✓ Highlights how and when specific behaviors may or may not be considered sexual harassment
   - ✓ Suggests that there are gender and cultural differences that may influence our perceptions of what behaviors are sexual harassment
   - ✓ Prescribes the role that supervisors and employees should play in preventing and responding to sexual harassment
   - ✓ Details either organizational-specific, if they are available, or generic complaint procedures.

Variations
1. Precede the small group discussions with a definition of sexual harassment and a review of laws, policies, procedures, and research detailing its prevalence. This can be done through a lecture or the use of the many excellent videos on the market. This provides participants with a knowledge base to enhance their discussion of the cases.

2. Require that each group develop and perform a role play to exemplify a possible next step or way to resolve the problem presented in its case. This fosters skill building.

3. Instead of using prepared cases, challenge each group to develop and discuss its own case that describes a workplace situation that may be considered sexual harassment.

Unwelcome sexual advances, requests for sexual favors, and other verbal or physical conduct of a sexual nature constitute sexual harassment when:

Quid Pro Quo Harassment

1. submission to such conduct is made either explicitly or implicitly a term or condition of an individual's employment;
2. submission to or rejection of such conduct by an individual is used as the basis for employment decisions affecting such individual; or

Hostile Work Environment

3. such conduct has the purpose or effect of unreasonably interfering with an individual's work performance or creating an intimidating, hostile, or offensive work environment.

Examples

1. Unwanted physical contact: touching a co-worker's shoulder
2. Gestures: puckering lips, making finger signs
3. Off-color jokes: need not be told directly to harassed employee, but just overhearing may be enough to create a hostile work environment in that employee's mind
4. Pictures: pin-ups of scantily clad individuals
5. Demeaning comments about women or men, terms of endearment, questionable compliments, generalities that lump women or men together as a group or denigrate them: "honey" or "You look hot."

Case 1

Joyce is a candidate for a position in a company that has an excellent reputation as a leader in its industry and very optimistic growth potential. In the first interview she had with Mark, who would be her direct supervisor should she obtain the job, Joyce felt that she presented herself very well and was confident that she was a strong contender for the job. Joyce was pleased when Mark called and told her that his boss, Peter, a vice-president in the company, now needed to meet her. Mark let her know that this was just a formality and, unless something went terribly wrong in her meeting with Peter, Mark would be offering her the position. Joyce was very excited at the likelihood that she would land this wonderful opportunity at a substantial salary increase from her prior job.

Dressed in her most professional business attire, Joyce arrived promptly for her meeting with Peter. At first, Peter was gracious and very professional, asking questions about her past experience, skills, educational background, and career aspirations. He then suggested that they go to lunch together so that they could continue to get to know each other better. After driving for about 30 minutes to a secluded country inn, Joyce began to feel nervous, but the conversation in the car had been about the position and Peter's expectations for the company's future. The hostess at the inn greeted Peter by name and indicated that his usual table was available. Peter offered Joyce a glass of wine, but she declined. He asked if she minded if he had one and then proceeded during the course of the lunch to consume the entire bottle.

As they were waiting for the check to arrive, Peter told Joyce that although he was very impressed with her qualifications, there was another strong candidate. However, Joyce was much more attractive than the other person, and if she played her cards right, she could use her appearance to her advantage. Peter asked her to consider spending the weekend with him to convince him that she was the better choice.

Is this an example of sexual harassment? What type? What should Joyce do?

Case 2

Melanie, the office secretary, frequently comes to work wearing revealing and provocative clothing. Both the men and women in the office joke about how well endowed she is and the men talk about how much they enjoy giving her work.

Alex, the director of the unit, has overheard the comments, but has refrained from participating in the conversations. He has observed Melanie's reactions and she seems to enjoy all the attention. In fact, he has observed her flirting with some of the men and asking them if they like her clothes.

Alex has also overheard the comments made by the women in the office. Some of the women think that the comments are getting out of hand and feel uncomfortable with all the talk about Melanie's body. Other women say that Melanie is getting the attention that she wants, and if it does not bother her, it is none of their business. A recent conversation between two secretaries has caused Alex to reconsider whether he needs to do something about the situation. The women were discussing a promotional opportunity that they predicted would go to Melanie since all the men think she is so attractive.

Is this an example of sexual harassment? What should Alex do?

Case 3

Ann and Frank have worked closely together for the past 6 months on a very intense business project. They have spent many hours late at night and on weekends together attempting to meet a demanding deadline. They have developed a close relationship and feel very comfortable with each other due to the fact that they spend more time together than they do with anyone else. They joke around a lot and often compliment each other.

Ann began to feel romantically attracted to Frank, but was hesitant to share her feelings while they were completing the project. If Frank was not interested, she feared it would make working together awkward and perhaps even quite difficult.

After the deadline passed and the project was over, Ann and Frank decided to go out to dinner to celebrate. During the dinner, Ann began to sense that Frank was also interested in her, but a little shy and maybe fearful of rejection, so Ann decided to make the first move. She touched his arm and said, "Now that the project is over, why don't we see if we can build a personal relationship." Frank smiled and said, "I would like that. I'll call you next week."

The next day the director of human resource asked to see Ann in her office. The director told Ann that she had received a sexual harassment complaint against her from Frank, who claimed that he has had to endure unwanted touching, suggestive compliments, and other inappropriate comments for the past 6 months. Now he claims that it has really gotten out of control because Ann has asked him out. Frank asked that Ann be transferred to another unit.

Is this an example of sexual harassment? What should Ann do? What is the appropriate action for the director of human resource to take?

Case 4

Joe is the secretary for the work unit. He thinks that many of his co-workers, both within the unit and in other departments in the company, believe he is gay even though he has not been public about his sexual orientation. One day at a staff meeting, the director, Harry, reports that the company is setting up a task force to discuss diversity issues. The task force will be discussing policies for homosexuals in the company, such as AIDS health issues and domestic partners benefits plans. Harry further reports that he has recommended Joe to represent their unit on the task force since Joe has much more experience and interest in issues that deal with people like him. Joe remains very quiet at the meeting, and although he thinks that some of his co-workers seem embarrassed, no one makes any comments. Harry moves on to the next item on the agenda.

Is this an example of sexual harassment? What should Joe do? What should Harry have done? What would you have done if you were at the meeting?

Case 5

Meredith has recently been disciplined for poor work performance. Bob, her supervisor, has documented a number of problems, including missed deadlines, errors in reports, and complaints from customers. He has warned Meredith that one more serious performance problem could result in her termination.

At a meeting with Sally, who is Bob's supervisor and the department head, Meredith tells Sally that Bob has been sexually harassing her for a long time and now he is trying to fire her. Meredith admits that her performance is suffering, but claims it is because she is working in such a hostile environment.

When Sally asks Meredith why she has not come forward sooner, Meredith says that she was fearful of retaliation, but now feels that she has no choice but to make a formal sexual harassment complaint and wants to know how to proceed.

Is this an example of sexual harassment? What should Sally tell Meredith to do?

MY BIGGEST PERFORMANCE BLOCK: IDENTIFYING AREAS FOR IMPROVEMENT*

Peter Dean and Martha Ray Dean

Peter J. Dean, *Ph.D., and* **Martha Ray Dean** *are principles in Excellence by Design (5506 East Sunset Road, Knoxville, TN 37914, 76173.1257@COMPUSERVE.COM), a consulting firm specializing in identifying and removing the blocks to exemplary individual and organizational performance. Peter is also head of the Human Resource Development Department at the University of Tennessee, editor of the book* **Performance Engineering at Work** *(IBST-PI Publications, 1994) and editor of the* **Performance Improvement Quarterly.** *Martha teaches curriculum development and student assessment in Philadelphia College of Bible's graduate program and has coauthored articles on training evaluation and nontraining performance improvement solutions.*

Overview

This activity introduces and sells the importance of nontraining performance improvement strategies to anyone unfamiliar with this concept. It also teaches participants about the *behavior engineering model* described by Thomas Gilbert in his well-known book *Human Competence: Engineering Worthy Performance* (McGraw-Hill, 1978). With this model, those individuals responsible for performance improvement can diagnose for, prioritize, and plan performance improvement interventions.

Suggested Time

30 minutes

Materials Needed

✓ Form A (Where Is My Biggest Performance Block?)

✓ Wall chart displaying Figure 4.1

✓ Large Post-it™ note for each participant

Procedure

1. Ask participants to think about their jobs and the question "Where is my biggest performance block?" (To avoid prejudicing responses, it is

*This activity was first described in Peter J. Dean, ed. 1994, *Performance Engineering at Work*, Batavia, IL: International Board of Standards for Training, Performance and Instruction.

1	2	3
4	5	6

Figure 4.1

important *not* to tell the participants that the activity will identify non-training performance interventions.)

2. Position a chart in front of the room that depicts six cells numbered 1 through 6, as in Figure 4.1. Make sure that the chart is large enough to accommodate all the anticipated entries.

3. Distribute Form A and a Post-it note to each participant. The prompt question on Form A is the following: "Improvement in which one of the following six areas would enable you to do your job better?" Participants are given six options. Each relates to one of six areas suggested by Gilbert's behavior engineering model.

   1. Information
   2. Resources
   3. Incentives
   4. Knowledge and skills
   5. Capacity for the job
   6. Security

4. Invite participants to write down the number of the response that they have chosen and place it on the chart you have displayed in the front of the room.

5. Next, label each cell as follows:

   1 = information
   2 = resources
   3 = incentives
   4 = knowledge/skill
   5 = capacity
   6 = security

Explain that each cell can dramatically influence performance. Emphasize that the first three cells (the top ones) represent factors in the environment in which the performer functions and that the next three cells (the bottom ones) represent factors related to the performer's individual characteristics.

6. Ask participants to comment on the results of the exercise as displayed on the chart. Point out that the clustering of Post-it™ notes reveals whether most of the participants perceive environmental factors (notes on top row) or individual factors (notes on bottom row) as blocking better performance. Introduce the discussion with questions such as the following:

   ✓ Why do you think there are the most notes in the *(insert number of most popular)* cell?

   ✓ What are the implications of having more data in the row related to the environment? (Note: *You should anticipate this outcome. The authors have conducted this activity with nearly 1000 participants from business and industry. Over two-thirds of participants have chosen environmental factors over individual factors.*)

   ✓ What are your organization's efforts to improve performance in light of these data? What are some specific ways in which information, resources, and incentives can be made more readily available? How can training, the matching of a person to a job, and job security be improved?

7. Use the data generated by the group to discuss the range of interventions that must be considered if individual and organizational performance is to be improved in their organizations. Point out that the results of this activity do not lessen the importance of training. In fact, training is more important than ever. Downsizing, job redesign, and the new jobs that are being created as the result of technical and scientific advancement all require training. Yet, with the increased emphasis on and investment in training, emphasize that it is more important than ever for performance improvement specialists to assure that the work environment will support the use of new skills and knowledge.

8. *(optional)* Conduct a cost–benefit analysis of different performance interventions. Ask this question: "How do we know that providing more information, resources, or incentives, for instance, will improve performance enough to make our efforts value added?"

Directions

✓ Answer the following question with one of the six options.

✓ Write the number of the option you selected on the Post-it™ note provided.

✓ Place the Post-it™ note on the chart in the cell with the number corresponding to the option you have selected.

Question

Improvement in which one of the following six areas would enable you to do your job better?

Answer options

1. Clear performance expectations and relevant feedback about the adequacy of your performance

2. Tools, resources, and materials to achieve your performance goals

3. Adequate pay and nonpay incentives made contingent on your performance

4. Systematically designed training that matches the requirements of your job

5. A match between your skills and the requirements of your job

6. Assurance of job security

5 INTERGALACTIC BUSINESS EXCHANGE: A NETWORKING SIMULATION

Raylie Dunkel

Raylie Dunkel *is the owner and director of The Brinkerhoff Group (PO Box 822, Freehold, NJ 07728, 908-462-7444, Raylie TBG@aol.com), a consortium of trainers and consultants. Raylie is the special projects coordinator of Quality New Jersey, corporate liaison of the New Jersey Association of Women Business Owners, and a member of the American Society for Training and Development. She is a delegate to the White House Conference on Small Business and the executive director of Northeast Technical Association and serves on the board of directors of the Jude Institute of New Jersey, Inc.*

Overview In the normal course of business almost everyone is expected to attend business meetings, organizational gatherings, or trade shows. The idea of being in a room full of strangers can cause panic in otherwise effective business men and women. The *Intergalactic Business Exchange* removes the typical constraints that participants usually place on themselves in a networking situation by asking them to play roles in a fantasy setting. This allows individuals to feel more comfortable about speaking in public, asking questions of others, and focusing on the real value of networking.

Suggested Time 60–90 minutes

Materials Needed ✓ Form A (Networking Tips)

✓ Form B (Role Play Descriptions)

✓ Form C (Networking Discussion Worksheet)

✓ Optional: To set the mood for the program, you may want to make up special name tags for the participants. The WingDings font on most computers will produce very odd characters that you can use for an International Intergalactic Language.

Procedure *Part I: Introduction*

1. Begin the program with a discussion about the purpose of networking. Solicit information from the audience with questions such as the fol-

24

lowing: Why do we network? What circumstances have you been in where you have networked? Were these formal or informal relationships? Business or personal interactions? What were the outcomes of the relationship? *Try to have the participants realize that networking is a natural event in our lives. We use it to find a new doctor, dentist, or day-care facility, a restaurant, or a piano teacher. We use networking as a normal course of business in finding vendors, developing sales leads, hiring personnel, or problem solving a situation.*

2. Distribute Form A. Discuss interesting points with the group.

Part II: Conducting the Intergalactic Business Exchange

3. Distribute one role-play description (using Form B) and, if desired, one Intergalactic name tag to each participant. If you have more participants than you have available occupations, have more than one person play some of the roles.

4. Give the group time to read the information. Let them know that they will have 15 minutes to "work the crowd" and ask others questions. Tell them that at the end of the time period they will be asked how many pieces of information they were able to gather. Remind them that direct contacts are not the only way to gather the needed information; referrals are perfectly legitimate contact points. Begin the networking simulation.

5. When 15 minutes have passed, ask everyone to find a seat. Ask them to tally up the

   Number of direct contacts that they made

   Number of people that they were able to refer

   Number of people to whom they were referred

6. Conclude the tallying exercise with the realization that networking is an elastic relationship that goes beyond the direct contacts that we make. The idea of being referred or making referrals is very important. The power of the networking experience comes from the second- and third-level referrals that can be derived out of any single contact.

Part III: Networking Discussion

7. This part of the activity brings the concept of the reach of information into focus as it applies to our daily lives. Have the participants resettle into small work groups. Round tables work well or use chairs drawn into circles. Try to keep the group size between four and six people. Distribute Form C. Ask everyone to fill in an individual goal. It can be business related (such as finding a new job or extending your number of business contacts) or it can be personal (finding a baby-sitter, a new physician or a lawyer). Have participants list possible strategies that they might use in accomplishing their goals. Participants take turns stating their goals; then one by one the group brainstorms a list of strategies and contacts that might be helpful for each individual.

8. Circulate around the room while the groups are working. Try to make sure that no one problem is monopolizing the group's time. Make sure that everyone has a turn to present his or her issue. Encourage individuals to continue discussions after the workshop if they have found someone who can be of direct assistance in meeting a participant's networking goal.

✓ Be prepared with a 1-minute speech about who you are, the nature of your business and the benefits of doing business with your company.

✓ If you are uncomfortable walking into a room, find someone that seems shy and talk to him or her. The person will be greatly relieved and you won't have to go through the stress of breaking into someone else's conversation. You will probably attract others to the group.

✓ Circulate! Spend only a few minutes talking to each person. Don't get into in-depth conversations. Move around the room. Try to meet as many people as possible. You can get back to individuals that are of interest to you at a later time.

✓ Always have business cards!

✓ Collect cards. Write down what happened on the back of the card. You may want to enter the cards into a data base when you get home or back to work.

✓ Always respond to the requests or promises made at the meeting as quickly as possible. Send a thank-you card for the meeting the next day. The longer you wait, the less effective the relationship experience.

✓ Stay in touch with people. Send notes, birthday cards, newspaper articles, invitations to organizational meetings that you think would be of interest, and so on.

✓ The exchange of information is not always equal. That is fine, because relationships tend to even out in the long run.

✓ You can plan a networking experience by deliberately searching out an individual who can supply the information that you need.

✓ Be prepared for unexpected or unplanned network opportunities. Always have business cards available.

✓ Don't presuppose anyone's reach of information. Everyone has family members and friends who might be able to extend your personal network.

✓ Only ask for things that are possible. Don't overwhelm your contacts.

Photocopy the following descriptions and cut them to form individual note cards on each occupation.

Builder and Contractor

You have a prefabricated building operation. Your specialty is building inexpensive industrial warehouse space. You can also build or remodel residential space to accommodate any physical peculiarities caused by integrating indigenous and foreign populations. You have to establish relationships with banking institutions who understand the requirements of construction loans, foreign currency exchanges, and revolving lines of credit. You would like to establish relationships with local architects, designers, and decorators because you want to offer finishing services to your customers without having to hire staff to conduct these services. You are looking to hire local help and will work with vocational schools to develop programs to train students or retrain adults in the skills necessary to your trade. Your ulcer is acting up and you are down to your last doses of medication because you did not have time for a check-up prior to moving. You need a real estate agent to find you some living quarters. You would like to rent for now and build later. You need to find decent day care for your 4-year-old twins and a part-time nanny. Your husband did not make the move with you but will be beaming up for weekends, and you need to connect with a travel agent who can handle all the arrangements, anywhere in the galaxy, because your husband travels and consults on many planets.

Architect

You specialize in remodeling projects to accommodate physical peculiarities caused by integrating foreign populations into indigenous housing stock. You excel at providing access for the multilimbed and tailed species that are now emigrating into newly established colonies. You have a wide background in the life styles of many different populations and the types of housing that they are used to. You would like to work with local builders and decorators because you view them as a market for your services. You are single and feeling lonely in your new environment and would like to meet other singles.

Trucker

You specialize in interplanetary shipping. You will ship anything anywhere in the universe. You have an excellent knowledge of intergalactic shipping regulations that can save customers a bundle of money on shipping costs. You can guarantee overnight delivery in this galaxy. No job is too small or too big. You can accommodate builders and manufacturers with large and bulky orders. Your business is growing rapidly and you have to add new drivers. You would like to be able to work with a temporary agency so that you don't have to keep people on payroll during slow times. You will also wrap and ship packages anywhere in the universe. You would like to find a local source for packaging supplies. You would like to throw a graduation party for your daughter. This will mean that you will be bringing in all her sorority sisters and their dates and will need to work out a reasonable arrangement for hotels for a few days.

Attorney

You specialize in intergalactic law, both commercial and domestic. You are a member of the bar on many planets and can represent clientele in absentia in their respective judicial systems, even though this means that you have to do a considerable amount of intergalactic travel. You would like to establish a good working relationship with a travel agent who knows how you like to travel. You like to play golf and are looking for a country club that will match you up with other club members in your handicap range. Your secretary and legal assistants did not want to relocate and you have to hire staff quickly. Speaking of relocating, you must find a proper prep school for your children and a dealership that will service your Mercedes Hovercraft XE, even though it was imported from another galaxy. You also have to find a caterer that specializes in intergalactic cuisine because so much of your entertaining is business-related.

Accountant

Numbers, numbers, numbers are all that you care about. You don't care which base system is used, you know them all. You have computer programs that can instantaneously calculate taxes on any planet in any star system. You specialize in intergalactic business accounting and will work with a company with locations on many different planets. You have a toothache.

Banker

The new colony that is springing up in this community is a boon to your business. You offer both commercial and personal banking services. You will help companies establish lines of credit and building expansion loans. You will help individuals mortgage new homes. You have been given a directive by your corporate office to make this branch the best that it can be! Your mandate is to offer liberal, but sound, loans to new and expanding businesses, to give this colony a good boost. You also believe that this is going to be a booming community, and you will be looking for land to build an expanded bank with the possibility of suburban satellites. You would like to corner the market on as many real estate projects as possible. You would like to work with the schools to promote a school banking project so that the children become familiar with your bank's services.

Employment Counselor and Headhunter

You are a generalist. You can supply companies with permanent or temporary help. You can work with clerical, management, or production-level employees. Your business is expanding and you are thinking of opening new offices that are in keeping with the newly expanded business community that is developing around you. You would like to print some snazzy new brochures and are looking for someone to help you design and print them. You are always interested in hearing about new ideas that will expand your business.

Manufacturer

You manufacture and distribute the best devices for high-technology manufacturing processes. You are interested in establishing relationships with local suppliers and subcontractors who can assist you in getting your product to market quickly. You need to construct warehouse and office space quickly so that you can get into production. You need to establish a rotating line of credit to purchase raw materials. You will need to connect with local shipping companies because you do not wish to establish your own shipping fleet at this time. The company must be able to ship to both local and intergalactic markets. (This company must know a lot about intergalactic tariffs, because your last shipper was costing you a fortune in unnecessary taxes.) It is important that the shipper have the ability to deliver overnight to your customers because most of them are using the just-in-time method of inventory control. You will be planning a large tour of the factory and a luncheon when the plant is finished. You need to staff the production force from local populations, even if they represent nonhuman species. There may be a problem of integrating the indigenous population with the management team that you are bringing in from the Earth-based and lunar company affiliates. Your wife wants to plan your daughter's wedding in your new home (that you have not located yet) because her relatives have never visited Mars and she thinks that it is a wonderful excuse to host a major family event.

Printer and Graphic Designer

You specialize in graphic design and printing for all sizes of companies. Your computerized printing plant can work with any format of material in any of the intergalactic languages. You offer automatic translation services to make your business clients adaptable to doing interplanetary business. You are familiar with regulations for labeling and safety at any location in the star system. Your motto is "No job is too big or too small or too far away." Now that business is growing, you would like to move the production closer to the new industrial park that is being developed. You would like this move to accommodate the expansion that you plan over the next 5 years. You have your eye on the new high-speed presses available back on Earth. You can get a great deal on one, but you have to provide your own shipping and handling.

Distributor and Vendor

You order, import, and distribute everything possible in your field. Your see a new boom coming with the influx of new businesses in the area. Because this is an outpost of civilization, you are an integral part of any type of business that uses your products. You are heavily dependent on the services of truckers and the communications and telephone network. You need to negotiate the best prices possible due to your heavy volume. Because you order from manufacturers all over the galaxy and ship all over the star system, you need to work with people who understand intergalactic tariff systems. You are also in the market for a new accountant. You see incoming business changing the way that you will be doing business, and you want to be able to negotiate the best tax breaks that you can. You plan to hire new personnel to keep up with the expanding business. They will have to be trained in customer service, because you believe that customer service is the lifeblood of your business. You utilize just-in-time practices and so do many of your customers. You would like to put together standard interactive video that you can use as a training tool for new hires. You find that all this business expansion is interesting and exciting, but it does cause havoc with your ulcer. You really should find a new doctor.

Telephone and Communication Sales

Communications is the name of the game in space, or at least that's what you tell your customers. You are the person who makes it possible for companies to deal in the interplanetary business arena in an instantaneous fashion. You make it as easy for someone to call into another star system as it is to call across the street or into the next crater. You have technicians that will service equipment anywhere in the newly developing network. Getting good help is always a problem, and you would like to work out a deal with the technical high school to train technicians for you. You also have an idea for an optical computer switching station. This will need funding, lab space, and production capabilities, but if you can get your work together you will be able to get into production quickly. You will need someone who can print the technical and promotional material in all the intergalactic languages.

Office Supplier

You are the Office Max of the stars. You can stock any business form known to humans and other beings. You can have material ordered in any language in the star system. Your computers and office furniture are ergonomically designed to accommodate any bodily form in the universe. With the growing demand that all the new building is placing on your business, you are looking for expanded warehouse and retail space. Your increased demand for shipping to other planets is making you look for a new trucker (the last one did not know enough about intergalactic tariffs and was costing you a fortune). You stock every type of computer known to humans and others. Service is what you are about. You want to have plenty of personnel around to handle customer requests, but the nature of your employment patterns makes you reliant on part-time workers.

Newspaper Publisher

You publish the only local newspaper on this colony. The new boom in business expansion can be a gold mine for you, but you have to capitalize on it. You have to convince the newcomers that public relations is as important here as it is on Earth. To make a dent in the new markets, you would like to hire a few special-feature reporters who can help new companies get the recognition that they need. You want the paper to have a fresh new look to keep up with the more sophisticated clientele that you see arriving daily. Perhaps putting some money into a new graphic design will be money well spent. You would also like to outsource the printing of the paper because the expanded version that you would like to publish is more than your equipment can handle. You really have to get quotes on new equipment versus outsourcing. You have to speak to a banker to find out if the bank will grant loans to expanding businesses. All this new business planning is very exciting, but it is giving you headaches, stomach pains, and a general feeling of anxiety. Maybe you ought to see a doctor.

Caterer and Restaurant Owner

Food. You love to cook it, no matter where it comes from in the universe. You have a fine reputation for innovative ideas and will accommodate any dietary need. You specialize in Intergalactic Cuisine. Corporate catering is a special part of your business because you know that foreign customers can be made to feel comfortable if presented with food that they find familiar. You often tell your business accounts that the way to their customers' wallets is at the dinner table. Make them comfortable with your hospitality, let them see that you will cater to their needs, and they will assume that you will take care of their business needs in the same manner. Your dining room reflects this caring for your customers, no matter where in the universe they are from. Your surroundings, your furniture, and your food make everyone or anything comfortable. Birthday parties, anniversaries, weddings, and special family occasions are important parts of your business. With locals bringing up so many relatives for a visit, their homes are usually not big enough to accommodate the crowds, and they turn to you for party planning. This puts pressure on you to keep coming up with fresh ideas. This is stressful, but you love it. For relaxation, you plan a number of getaways for yourself and your family to quiet retreats whenever you can. You need to find a new travel agent, because your last one went on a junket to Pluto and never came back.

Interior Designer

The new influx of people and business is a boon for your business. You can handle both commercial and residential work. You can work with any design scheme or pocketbook. You know that today's small customer could be tomorrow's large customer. You also know service. With so many businesses moving here, customers don't have the time to pick and chose all their decorating details, and you are happy to help them. You know how to help businesses make their intergalactic customers feel comfortable in furniture designed to fit any type of body, no matter where in the universe it is from. You also know how to make the relocation process easier by helping families to create a home away from home. You do need to form a good working relationship with a trucker and mover, especially someone who knows intergalactic shipping codes and tariffs. You would like to establish a revolving line of credit with the bank to make your sporadic buying easier to handle. You have to find a good day-care center for your son and daughter; a facility with flexible hours that fosters a feeling of cooperation with the diverse backgrounds of children in this colony.

Computer Consultant

A newly emerging business community is forming up here in the stars and its members all run on computers. Computers to run the manufacturing plants, computers to take pictures, computers to communicate all over the galaxy. What a gold mine! Your business is really growing, but good business practices must be followed to keep up with the expansion. You have to be careful to get business consulting assistance to keep your operations strong. You would like to expand some of the services you offer and provide customized programming to meet specific business needs. You would also like to work with the schools to provide all their computer needs: hardware, software, and service. You need to work with a good placement firm to locate good sales and service people. You are always developing new promotional materials and know that they have to be printed in all the new languages spoken up here.

Shared Office Complex Manager

What a concept and what a time to be in business here! With all these new businesses opening up, you are in a boom economy. You can provide services to consultants, professionals, and sales representatives in part-time secretarial work, phone answering services, and general clerical work. Anyone who needs office or conference space on a limited basis is a target for your services. You can house businesses while they expand and support businesses while they are building new space. This meeting is crawling with prospective clients. You would like to form a sales lead group with a personnel placement company, builder, contractor, telephone services, and so on. Anyone who is in touch with companies that are forming (lawyers, accountants) or who might have to put clients into temporary space is a good contact for you.

Trainer and Consultant

You look out at the new business developing around you and see potential business. Transitional change workshops, customer services, business management, and technical training are but a few of the subjects that you work in. You would like to team up with other professionals, especially in the vocational school and communication areas. You need to work with a printer to get your materials compiled in a professional manner. You are always developing new job aids, and a graphic designer willing to work on a project basis would take a part of the workload off of your shoulders. Does anyone around here offer part-time secretarial help? Your move up here has wreaked havoc with your back. You are in pain and cannot sleep at night, and your doctor is a whole star system away.

Travel Agent

With everyone coming and going all over the universe, the services of a good travel agent are always welcome. You specialize in business travel, but delight in handling private accounts. You know the pressure that everyone works under and find it rewarding to help someone plan a relaxing getaway. You will organize whole companies that are moving or help with plans for a family reunion. This is important due to all the expansion in the colony. Every family seems to be planning special events up here. You know that your relationship with local hotels and event planners is an important arm of your business expansion and are always looking to foster these types of relationships. You also recognize the increase in the diverse populations coming here from so many outlying star systems. You would like to have brochures printed in these languages to capture some of this business. You have just found out that you were pregnant before you moved here and need to find a good doctor. You are the kind of person that likes to plan ahead and therefore would like to begin the process of interviewing day-care centers or finding live-in help.

Event Planner

Sometimes it seems that life is one big party and you love it. Weddings, family gatherings, and special events are what you enjoy planning most. However, you know that the big bucks are in corporate functions: trade shows, conferences, meetings, and retreats. You will plan any event from beginning to end. Your relationships with vendors, suppliers of tables, chairs, linen, and the like, are crucial. You also have to connect with hotel, conference space, travel agents, and entertainers. Being new in the middle of a star system is exciting and challenging. You have to connect with new services quickly so that you can begin to market yourself. Speaking of marketing, you need cards and brochures yourself. Is there a printer here who customizes balloons? You would like to find the hot travel agent on this outpost, because you will probably need to make travel arrangements for clients. Besides, travel agents know who is planning a big event, business or social, and there might be opportunities to work together. Because you run around all the time, you would like to rent space in a shared office environment so that someone can answer your phone when you are not available. You also have to get to the high school and talk to the principal. Your twin daughters are giving you a really hard time about the move, and your know that the adjustment into the new school system will be difficult. Sophomore girls transported into the new universe—how inconvenient!

Commercial and Personal Photographer

You are a camera whiz, and you really make people look good. You recognize the importance of photography in people's lives. Special events should be photographed as a part of life's passages. You also know the importance of photography in business. New product development, annual reports, and promotional materials all need documentation. So do people, which is why you offer quick and inexpensive intergalactic passport pictures processed while the customer waits. New computerized photography makes a quick turnaround time easy to accomplish, and you can capitalize on this in your advertising. You pride yourself on keeping up on the latest improvements and consider the computer salesperson almost a business partner. You would like to expand your business along with the business and residential community by establishing yearly photography programs in the schools and nursery schools. You will also work with schools to provide coverage for plays and sporting events. You would like to hire a few part-time assistants, perhaps even a few students at the technical school. Speaking of school, you should make an appointment to meet with the high school principal about your son.

Nursery School Director

You love your job here on the colony. You cater to a diverse population of children and help them to feel comfortable with the new and strange-looking playmates. You feel that in some way you are contributing to universal peace by teaching all these little children to get along with each other. Your business is growing as a result of this attitude. You are completely accommodating to the new populations here. You know that there is a lot of stress put on families when they relocate, and you try to make the transitions as easy as possible on the children. You will accommodate long working hours of the parents through innovative programs. You will help families with private in-home child-care services. In fact, you see this as a way to expand your business and would like to work with an employment agency in a joint venture. You have the ability to work well with other people's children and would like to continue expanding your business opportunities.

High School Principal

As if high schoolers don't have enough problems already! Bringing a group of transported kids into a new outpost of civilization is going to be a great challenge to you and your staff. You know that you will need some adjunct services to ease the transition for the families that are moving here. Perhaps some special programs in managing change, special events, and parental get-togethers could help your students and staff. You also have some extensions and renovations to complete on the building. You know that the communication equipment needs upgrading and you have to put in new computer labs. You will have to furnish all the new rooms and order office equipment. You have to find some vendors here that can take over your textbook orders. You also have to settle your own family into the new environment. They will be joining you in a few months, and you have to find and furnish a place to live.

Vocational School Director

With all the new businesses opening, here you see a transition in the wind. You would like to offer more industrial training courses to the business community. You already have the machine shops, computer labs, and industrial cooking programs in place. You would like to offer supportive training to any new business that is developing in the galactic community. You have received supportive grant money from the government to assist manufacturers in their transitions. You will have to connect with the businesses that need training and the consultants that can offer training in specific areas, because you are not going to hire new staff for each additional program. The board of education has given you money to put in an up-to-the-minute Communications Lab. You have heard that there is a communications business coming into the area and you would love to subcontract with them, because you are looking for technical expertise and advice.

Dentist

Its amazing—medical technology has made it so easy and painless to treat dental problems, but people still don't take care of their teeth. With all the new businesses opening up, you know that there is great potential to develop relationships with new families. You also know that people still ignore their teeth until they hurt. You would love to put some portable offices into schools, clinics, and industrial settings to make it easier for people to take care of their teeth. You would also like to start awareness programs in the nursery and elementary schools. You will need to print charts and brochures to interest the children. You would love to see a dental technology program started at the vocational school. You will need a new accountant to help you keep track of the growing business that you foresee.

Doctor

If it's a body, you can treat it. Intergalactic medicine was your specialty in medical school. You are very interested in this position because so many different populations will be coming together to live and work in a new setting. You would like to see a walk-in clinic set up, with satellites in the commercial centers to help workers with work-related injuries. Workplace medicine is important to you. You would like to see business owners sponsor awareness programs that will keep this new and divergent work force healthy and productive. You are especially concerned about spreading diseases among various species and feel that education is one way to prevent problems. You would like to print brochures in the intergalactic languages to distribute in your office and at the satellites when they are constructed and staffed. You would like to find trainers to collaborate with you on workplace educational programming. You will also have to work with an employment agency to staff the expanding medical treatment facilities. You are interested in working with the schools at all levels to establish preventive and well-child programs. On the personal side, your spouse would like to build a home befitting your position and income.

Hotel and Conference Center Manager

With everyone flying in, setting up new businesses, and needing temporary living space, you see great potential as well as great problems. First, you need to build special apartments that can be rented on a short-term basis while people are in transition. You will need to have them fully furnished and equipped. Renting your hotel rooms should not be a problem, but you would like people to know about your conference and party space as well. Teaming up with a party planner or caterer would be a great idea. You also need some splashy brochures made up to advertise the facility. Heavy traffic places great wear and tear on the carpets and furniture. They need constant updating and replacement. You would like to work with a decorator who will handle that aspect of the business for you. Due to the high volume of food and beverage that your patrons consume, you have to find a vendor that will work well with you, especially during the holidays. You know that general tourism will be up as the star system becomes a hot vacation spot. You would like to work out some interesting tour packages and events for guests once they get here.

NETWORKING DISCUSSION WORKSHEET

Your individual networking goal is to

_____

_____

What are possible strategies that you might take to reach your goal?

1. _____

2. _____

3. _____

4. _____

5. _____

What contacts might be of assistance to you?

1. _____

2. _____

3. _____

4. _____

5. _____

6. _____

OPENING WINDOWS™: ACCELERATED LEARNING EXERCISES FOR THE NEW USER

Dawn Adams

Dawn Adams *has worked in the area of training for 12 years as a computer software training developer and instructor for such companies as Aetna Life and Casualty, Andersen Consulting, AT&T, and her own company, TechKnowledgy, Inc. She currently applies accelerated learning techniques to the computer-based training and multimedia-based courseware that she creates. Dawn can be reached at TechKnowledgy, Inc., 107 Edgedale Court, Kernersville, NC 27284, (910) 996-5290 or 73534.254@compuserve.com.*

Overview   Here are three quick exercises that you can use either separately or together for introductory training to *Windows*. The first exercise helps learners to visualize the directory file structure, the second demonstrates the file-naming convention, and the third illustrates how to search for file names.

Suggested Times: Exercise 1: Drawing the File System (25 minutes)

Exercise 2: The Computer Ruler (20 minutes)

Exercise 3: File Search Poker (20 minutes)

Materials Needed   ✓ White paper and colored markers for drawing a file system

✓ Form A (Drawing the File System)

✓ Form B (The Computer Ruler)

✓ Form C (File Search Poker)

✓ Several sets of 38 cards (enough for one-half of the participants) for the File Search Poker exercise

Exercise 1: Drawing the File System

Overview   The purpose of this exercise is for the learner to discover that the file structure of *Windows* is very similar to that of a cleverly constructed warehouse. All files are organized by type, and no two file systems are alike. Conduct this exercise as part of a discussion on using the file manager.

Procedure 1. Explain to the participants that they are going to be receiving a shipment of files that need to be stored. However, the warehouse does not yet exist. The first task is to draw a set of blueprints for the warehouse.

2. Divide the groups into teams of two or three. Distribute paper, markers, and Form A to each team. *Note:* It is helpful if you use the same directory structure that exists on the PCs that the participants will be using for the course.

3. Present directions and warehouse rules using Form A. Tell the group that they will have 15 minutes to make a blueprint for the new file warehouse. Answer any questions that the participants have about the exercise before they begin.

4. Have two groups bring up their blueprints and discuss their solutions. Ask the class if there are any other different arrangements and discuss those possibilities.

5. Debrief the exercise by explaining that a computer's hard disk is like a big empty warehouse. The disk is broken out into rooms called directories. The main hall of the warehouse is called the root directory or just the root.

Exercise 2: The Computer Ruler

Overview The purpose of this exercise is to illustrate the Windows 8.3 file-naming convention. Use the computer ruler on Form B to demonstrate the naming concept and then as a reference tool for practice.

Procedure 1. Distribute Form B to each participant.

2. Explain that every file on a computer has a name that consists of a first name, a middle initial, and a last name.

3. Explain that, just as a ruler has 12 inches, *Windows* uses 12 characters to represent a file name. The first 8 inches are used for a file's first name and the last 3 inches are used for the last name. All *Windows* files have a . (dot) for a middle initial and it is usually found in the ninth inch.

4. Demonstrate one or two correct file names using all 12 characters on one of the blank rulers.

5. Ask the learners what would happen if the first name was less than 8 "inches" long? Demonstrate using the ruler. Explain that *Windows* is smart enough to recognize first names that are anywhere between 1 and 8 characters long. It is not necessary to use all 8 characters.

6. Refer to the last name, known as the file extension. Every file must have a last name, which can have up to three characters.

7. Next explain the rules for what characters *Windows* allows in names. Explain that there can be no spaces in either the first or last name but that they can use the __ (underscore). Numbers can be used as well.

8. Using the ruler, show the participants an example of a file name with a space in the name. Ask if this name is acceptable.

9. Ask the participants to (a) identify various correct and incorrect file names and (b) create names for new computer files. Use Form B as a reference tool.

10. After 5 minutes of individual work, ask participants to team up with someone else. Challenge the teams to practice coming up with names that will "stump your partner."

11. Debrief the exercise by explaining that this naming convention is called 8.(dot)3 and is a requirement for naming any files that are put in *Windows*. Applications such as word processing or spreadsheet files all use this convention. Explain that, although learners may occasionally encounter software that allows them to use longer names, an 8.3 file name is still the standard.

Exercise 3: File Search Poker

Overview This exercise is useful for explaining and demonstrating how to use the * wild-card character and the File Manager Search feature to search for file names.

Procedure 1. Ask participants whether they have ever played poker using a wild card. Find a volunteer to explain what the wild card allowed them to do (match anything in your hand).

2. Explain that *Windows* has a wild card as well, the character *, that allows the computer to match characters in file names.

3. Question the participants on their experiences filing something away and then not being able to find it. Let one or two participants tell their stories.

4. Ask if it would be convenient to be able to tell the computer to find a file even if you did not know the whole name or where the file was. Explain that the *Windows* wild card (*) does just that.

5. Tell the participants that they are going to play File Search Poker. Pair up the participants into two-person teams and give each pair a set of 38 cards needed in the exercise. [Prepare, in advance, several sets of 38 3 by 5 inch cards. Each set will contain 26 cards with each letter of the alphabet (A–Z), 10 cards with each of the numerals 0–9, a card with an asterisk (*), and a card with a black dot.] Also, pass out Form C and explain the directions. Give the first search problem and deal the winning (correct answer) hand as an example.

6. Debrief the exercise by putting up a sheet with the correct answers for the problems. Ask if there are any different answers and discuss them as a class. Go on to explain how the Search All Subdirectories feature can be used to search an entire hard disk. Using this box is like being able to look at everyone's cards.

7. Give the participants time to practice using the * and the Search All Subdirectories feature.

Warehouse Rules

✓ Only one front door, no back door, and no windows.

✓ You must be able to get from the front door to any main room without going through another room.

✓ You can group similar files in rooms off the main rooms.

Shipping Manifest

Main Rooms	Files
WP (word processing)	January newsletter February newsletter Letter to Mom
DB (database)	Database queries Database reports
SS (spreadsheet)	1995 budget 1995 actuals 1996 budget
DRAW (graphics)	Pictures for January newsletter Pictures for February newsletter
DOS	System software
COMM	Communications software
TERM	Terminal emulation software

THE COMPUTER RULER

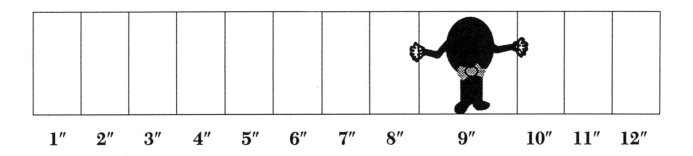

1"   2"   3"   4"   5"   6"   7"   8"   9"   10"   11"   12"

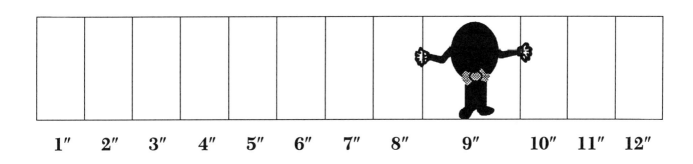

1"   2"   3"   4"   5"   6"   7"   8"   9"   10"   11"   12"

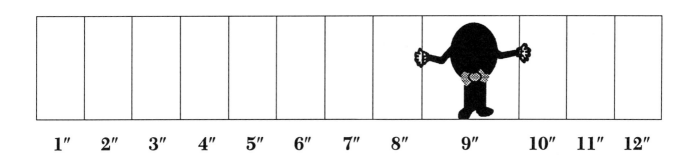

1"   2"   3"   4"   5"   6"   7"   8"   9"   10"   11"   12"

✓ For each of the file search problems given next, have one person deal the cards selected from your set of 38 cards that will give a solution. The other person will check it.

✓ If both agree that the answer is correct, write down the answer and continue to the next problem. Switch off dealing and checking until you are done.

✓ You have 10 minutes.

1. All file names that begin with _____ the letter A and have an extension of DOC

2. All file names that have an _____ extension of TXT

3. All file names that start_____ with 95

4. All file names that start with 123 _____ and have an extension of XLS

5. All file names that begin with _____ the letter D

7
THE COCKTAIL PARTY:
MEETING PEOPLE ON THE INSIDE

Carol Harvey

Carol Harvey, *Ed.D., is an associate professor of management and marketing at Assumption College (550 Salisbury St., Worcester, MA 01615-0005, 508-767-7459). A former manager with the Xerox Corporation, she is the coauthor of* **Understanding Diversity: Readings, Cases and Exercises** *(HarperCollins, 1995).*

Overview This activity increases participant awareness of the the internal similarities that exist among a diverse group of people. Intended as an opening activity for diversity training workshops, *The Cocktail Party* works well both for groups who have never met before and those who interact on a daily basis. It can also be used as a social icebreaker for any training session.

The Cocktail Party is designed to accomplish four goals:

1. Relieve the anxiety that people bring to diversity training
2. Provide instant interaction among the participants
3. Begin the session on a positive note
4. Provide the trainer with feedback as to how the participants really feel about this sensitive subject

This exercise works best when there are some dimensions of difference and diversity in the group. Usually, there are at least gender, ethnicity, and age differences. However, it is even more effective when there are some additional visible dimensions of diversity represented, such as race and/or physical challenges.

Suggested Time 30–45 minutes, depending on group size

Materials Needed ✓ Name tags
✓ Pencils and 10 index cards for each participant
Note: *Keep an additional stack of index cards nearby if necessary (see verbal instructions).*

Procedure

1. Explain to the participants that they are to imagine that they are attending a cocktail party. Their task is to "work the room" by meeting people and discovering something that they each have in common. Tell them that, even if they work with each other or already know each other, they will be getting acquainted on a different basis.

2. Be sure that everyone is wearing a name badge and has been supplied with 10 index cards and a pen or pencil.

3. Clear the space or move to a room where the participants can walk around just as they would at a cocktail party. *Note:* If you have physically challenged individuals who are, for example, confined to wheelchairs, it is not necessary to make any special arrangements for them. As long as your location is accessible to them, they will be fine.

4. Once that everyone is standing and is ready to begin, read the following instructions:

    Assume that you are attending a cocktail party. Just as it would be at a party, your goal is to meet people with whom you have something in common. You will have 15 minutes to do so. However, the difference here is that this common experience, background, preference, or whatever, cannot relate to anything visible. For example, the fact that you both have brown eyes won't do.

    You are to make conversation with another guest until you discover something in common that you two share. For example, you could discover that you both own German shepherds or go to the same dentist. When this happens, you have made a match and each of you should write down what you both have in common on one of your index cards.

    Then move to another person to try to discover another commonality, which will be recorded on a second index card. The same common experience cannot be reused for another guest. For example, if you discover that you attended the same college as another participant, college is no longer a usable match between you and another party guest.

    If you use all your index cards, additional ones are available. Keep circulating until time is called.

    Are there any questions? Let the party begin.

5. Sometimes people are awkward at first, but they quickly catch on and enjoy this interaction. Allow the party to continue for approximately 15 minutes. If the group is large (more than 20 participants), you may want to allow up to 20 to 25 minutes for additional discoveries.

6. As people mingle, observe their interaction patterns. At first, people tend to talk only to people in close physical proximity or to those who are somewhat like them. For example, people from the same departments and of the same age or gender tend to approach each other first. Fortunately, after a few minutes these possibilities exhaust themselves, and the guests begin to approach new and different people.

Although the directions say nothing about winning by filling the most index cards, some people become very competitive, while others just drift from person to person, enjoying their individual conversations.

7. Function as an observer in a nonobtrusive way. What body language is immediately apparent? Are people fidgeting? Do they appear uncomfortable asking others somewhat personal, often probing questions? (Usually, participants appear quite comfortable and motivated as soon as they have made their first successful match.) Do they appear to be enjoying themselves at the party? How close do people tend to stand to each other?

   Note: *It is not recommended that you remove any members from the group to act as observers. Part of this exercise's dynamic is that all members of the group participate on a level basis.*

8. Call time as necessary.

9. Invite the participants to sit down to discuss the results of this exercise. Effective discussion questions include but certainly are not limited to the following list:

   Did you enjoy the party? Why? (Participants often cite liking the structure that forced them to talk to many other people.)

   What did you dislike? (Usually, someone will cite the limited time, but extending the time really serves no purpose.)

   What surprised you about this experience? (Answers here vary.)

   What really happened here? (How did you feel when you discovered that you shared a common experience with another guest? These are always positive answers, and the common experience is often surprising to the participants.) Provide your observations of the people dynamics that occurred during the party.

   How can you relate this exercise to having a work force, team, or department that is composed of people who have visible differences? (Gender, race, age, and ethnic differences are often cited as being barriers to open communication, team development, informal interactions such as eating together, social conversations, and so on. Judgments are made about people based on their visible differences and on the assumption that they are different when no attempt was made to find similarities.)

10. Encourage each participant to anonymously write on one additional index card what he or she has learned from or how he or she feels about this experience. This allows the more quiet members of the group to be heard. Encourage honesty and assure the participants that this information is only to help you to conduct a more effective training session. Collect the cards and use the feedback to provide yourself with a clearer understanding of this group's true thoughts and feelings about diversity. If appropriate, share a summary of the cards with the group at a later point.

PATHWAYS: A TECHNIQUE TO REINFORCE A TRAINING SESSION

Jane LeClair

Jane LeClair, *Ed.D., is president of the Adult Learning Connection (3460 Stanford Drive, Baldwinsville, NY 13027, 315-635-7595), a consulting firm specializing in adult learning and development seminars for the business community. Jane is also a job coach and organization development specialist with Niagara Mohawk Power Corporation. She is a lecturer at numerous colleges and has authored* **Humanism in a High Tech Setting** *(1989), and* **Motivation in Nuclear Training** *(1990).*

Overview Most educators and trainers would agree that one of the most important aspects in a learning session is reinforcement of the presented material. Active reinforcement of a learning session serves two functions: (1) It allows learners the opportunity to interact with the subject material, and (2) it causes the presented material to stick in the minds of learners through immediate use. *Pathways* serves both functions. It is an end-of-session game that requires active participation as learners negotiate a serpentine path and pause to answer questions relating directly to the presented material.

Suggested Time 30 minutes, depending on group size

Materials Needed ✓ One large die

✓ Cardboard poster-sized cutouts that, when arranged on the floor, form a serpentine pathway (see Form A). Cutouts are printed with question symbols or movement instructions or are left blank.

✓ Master sheet with training questions and answers or individual question and answer cards.

✓ A nominal prize for the winner.

Procedure 1. Once the pathway is laid out on the floor, individuals or teams roll the die and move forward from the starting space, seeking to be the first to reach the finish line and win. Along the way are symbols representing the major topics from the presented material.

2. If a player (or team representative) lands on a symbol, a related question from the master sheet is asked. If answered correctly, the team gets another turn. If a player (or team representative) lands on a space containing movement instructions, the instructions are followed. Play continues until the finish line is reached and a nominal prize is awarded.

Variations *Pathways* can be modified to any situation. When the learning area is large, the path can be constructed such that individuals can act as the playing pieces and walk along the path, as described. Smaller settings may require the game to be played on a flip chart or poster-sized board using stickers for markers. It may also be adapted to smaller-sized board games for multiple-group use.

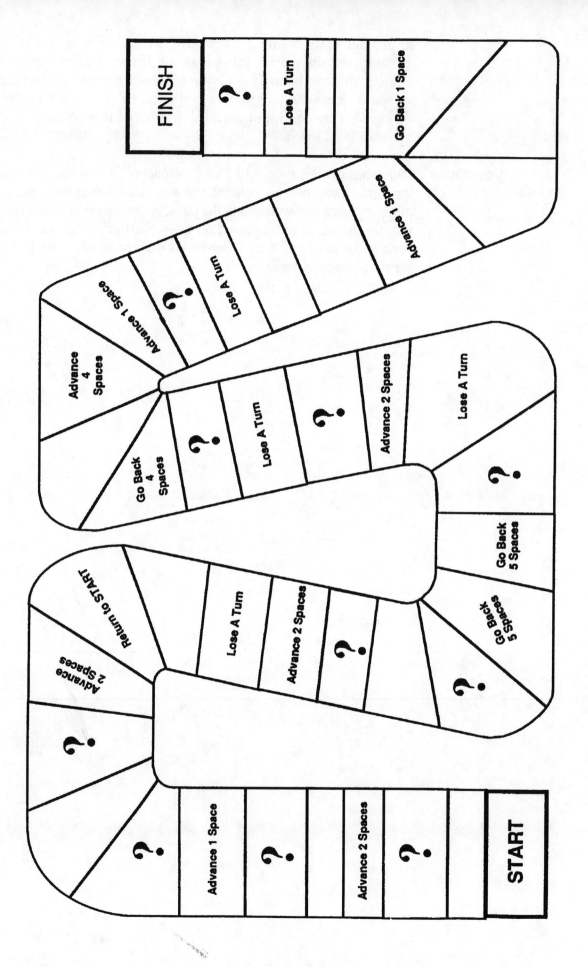

CAREER EXPLORATION: FINDING THE RIGHT CAREER FOR YOU

Leigh Mundhenk

Leigh G. Mundhenk *is an independent training and organizational development consultant (2 Aster Court, Doylestown, PA 18901, 215-340-0556) who specializes in change management and career planning with special focus on organizations and individuals affected by restructuring and layoffs. Leigh is affiliated with Drake, Beam, Morin, Inc., and Bucks County Community College. She is also the vice-president for Special Interest Groups for the Delaware Valley Chapter of the American Society for Training and Development.*

Overview   Looking for a new career? Nervous about networking? This training activity gives participants an opportunity to expand their thinking in making career choices and learn techniques designed to help them network for information. You can use *Career Exploration* either alone or as a preliminary workshop to a series on changing careers or job search skills. Although the activity can accommodate a group varying in size from 8 to 20, it works best with 12 to 16 people. This group size is large enough to be able to share resources and ideas, while still maintaining positive interaction among the participants. The activity also works best if participants come from different occupational backgrounds.

Suggested Time   90 minutes

(Note: *The time will vary depending on the number of participants. If the group is large, sections 17 to 19 can be eliminated or covered as a lecturette, depending on time constraints.*)

Materials Needed   ✓ Form A (Informational Interview Questions)

✓ Newsprint, markers, tape, flip chart

Procedure   1. Tell participants that this activity will provide them with a career exploration process that can help them find meaningful and rewarding work.

2. Explain that learning about careers comes from conducting library research and interviewing people who have careers that interest

them. Add that they will start by learning how to conduct informational (or networking) interviews and that, as part of this process, they will learn how to conduct a 1-minute introduction of themselves. Tell participants to begin by getting to know about one another; have each person introduce himself or herself using the following format:

✓ Name

✓ Where you grew up

✓ Where you went to school and what you studied

✓ A brief description of your career history

✓ A few things you have enjoyed about your work

✓ An idea or two about what career you are thinking of pursuing

✓ A final question asking the interviewee if she or he knows anyone in the field of work that interests you most

3. Introduce yourself, using the preceding format, to model how these introductions should take place.

4. Pair up participants. Ask each participant to take a turn giving a self-introduction to his or her partner. Encourage the listening partner to act naturally and respond where appropriate.

5. Create new pairs and repeat the mutual introduction process. Do this several times so that each participant meets at least six people.

6. Ask participants to listen carefully to the introductions and jot down the names of three to four people that they would like to interview later in the workshop who work in fields of possible interest.

7. Show how the networking process develops by drawing the following diagram on a flip chart and stating that the average person knows 200 people, each of whom know 200 people, and so on.

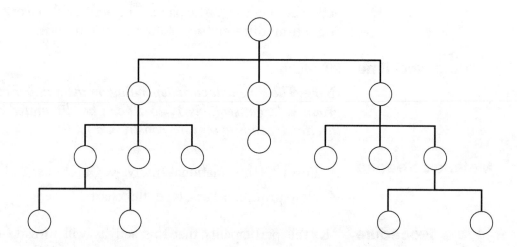

8. Tell participants that they should start with primary contacts, especially people who know others who can refer them to others in their field(s) of interest.

9. Form groups of fours and ask participants to brainstorm a list of potential contacts that they know (physicians, accountants, friends, and so on). Ask them to write their list on newsprint and post it on the wall when they are done.

10. Ask everyone to read each list to get ideas about whom they should initially contact.

11. State that when making contact with referrals from primary contacts it is helpful to mention the referring person and why that person thought the referral could be helpful. State that the objective is to get a brief 15- to 20-minute interview with the referral to ask him or her questions about his or her career. Since these contacts are usually made on the phone, urge participants to be brief and to the point, using the self-introduction discussed earlier.

12. Discuss the importance of having a well-planned interview that provides the information the participants need to make informed decisions.

13. Distribute Form A and state that these are some questions to consider asking. Point out that questions should not probe for information available from printed or on-line sources, but should be focused more on the interviewee's personal knowledge of the field.

14. Ask participants to work independently to develop and write a list of six to eight questions, using Form A as a guide, that they would want answers to in helping them to learn more about a particular career.

15. Divide the group in half by counting off "1, 2." Ask members of group 1 to choose a person from group 2, based on their self introductions, to interview. Pair up the remaining mismatched people, stating this role play can help them discover things about new opportunities that they may never have considered.

16. Ask participants to interview one another using their planned questions. After 10 minutes, ask members of group 2 to choose a person from group 1 that they wish to interview, and repeat the process.

17. Reconvene the whole group to discuss how the interviews have gone, asking for questions and comments.

18. In addition to informational interviews, state that there are a number of printed and on-line sources to obtain additional career information, such as salary ranges, training requirements, opportunities, professional associations, and typical career paths.

19. Ask participants what sources have been helpful to them in the past and make a list on a flip chart. Mention these resources if the participants have not already done so:

   ✓ Books on various careers (in library or bookstore)

   ✓ Government publications: *Dictionary of Occupational Titles*
   Guide for Occupational Exploration
   Occupational Outlook Handbook

✓ Computer programs (in libraries and college career centers) *SIGI PLUS*^R
   DISCOVER

✓ Periodicals and professional journals

✓ Newspapers

✓ Business journals

20. Ask participants from group 1 to again pair up with their interviewees to conduct a discussion on how to begin to learn more about their careers. Ask interviewees to serve as mentors, providing guidance, information, and direction where possible. Ask interviewers to work with their mentors to develop a plan for conducting informational interviews and using other information sources. After 10 minutes, ask group 2 to work with their mentors in the same manner.

21. Reconvene the whole group and ask each person to state something that they have learned that will be helpful in their career exploration process. Ask volunteers to share ideas as to how they plan to begin the process.

22. Close by stating that finding work that is based on individual interests and needs is an important and satisfying goal to attain. State that it may take hard work and time to achieve this goal, but the lifetime rewards make the effort truly worthwhile.

INFORMATIONAL INTERVIEW QUESTIONS

1. What kinds of growth and new directions are you experiencing in your field?

2. How is the health of the field?

3. Describe the specific strengths and/or skills needed to be successful in your field.

4. What publications could you read to learn more about this field?

5. What organizations or meetings could you attend or join to learn more about this field?

6. What has made you successful in your career? What things did you do to become successful?

7. What are the challenges facing people in this field?

8. What is your perspective on the needs and problems of people in this field?

9. How can you best prepare for this career?

10. Why did you choose this career?

11. What rewards do you get from your work?

12. Would you choose this career again?

HIVIAL PURSUIT: A KNOWLEDGE ASSESSMENT GAME*

Gwynne Sigel

Gwynne Sigel *is project coordinator of Educators Learning about Children with HIV and drug exposure (ELCHADE), University of Pennsylvania, GSE-CSSC, 3700 Walnut Street, Philadelphia, PA 19104-6216, 215-573-2990, Gwynnes@nwfs.gse.upenn.edu. ELCHADE is a four-year national training project that conducts four-day workshops to prepare educational staff to work with children affected with HIV and drug exposure in the regular classroom.*

Overview   Looking for a fun way to review potentially tedious learning material? This training activity derives its inspiration from a very popular board game and can be easily adapted to fit a wide variety of topics. Just separate your informational content into seven distinct categories, write down questions for each of these categories, distribute answer sheets to teams of participants, and let the games begin!

Suggested Time   60 minutes

Materials Needed   ✓ One pie-shaped game board (seven sections to match seven categories) and color-coded pie pieces for each team
✓ Form A (Answer Sheet)
✓ Form B (Game Questions)
✓ Form C (Game Answers)
✓ One set of prizes for the winning team

Procedure   1. Tell the participants that you are going to provide them with a fun and easy way of reviewing their knowledge about HIV. Stress that this cooperative activity allows team members to teach each other as they review the material that they have just learned.

2. Divide the group into teams of equal distribution. Teams should not exceed 10 members, and smaller teams of 5 work best.

*HIVial Pursuit is an adapted version of an exercise developed by the California Nurses Association.

58

3. Distribute one blank answer sheet (Form A) and one set of game questions (Form B) to each team.

4. Tell the group that you are giving them several questions about HIV. Working together with other team members, they will have 20 minutes to try to answer the questions using the answer sheet provided.

5. Encourage each team to try to answer as many questions in the allotted time as they can. If they are unsure of an answer to a particular question, instruct them to write "unknown" on the answer sheet.

6. Once the teams have had a chance to work through the questions, each group will have a chance to answer a question from one of seven designated categories that it believes it can answer correctly for the group.

7. If correct, the answering team gets to fill in the appropriate section of the pie board with one its pie pieces. (For example, if the team answers a question from the epidemiology category correctly, it fills in the section called epidemiology on the big game board.) Then the next team takes a turn.

8. If incorrectly answered, the next team gets to answer that question or another of its choice.

9. Once a question is answered correctly, no other team can use it.

10. Only one color pie piece (category) per game board (that is, a team cannot answer two questions about transmission, for example).

11. The first team to fill in its pie board wins.

12. Award prizes to the winners.

13. Distribute the master sheet of questions and answers (Form C) to all participants.

Variations
1. Give each team its own game board and otherwise play the game exactly as described. The first team to fill its pie board wins.

2. When giving teams time to work through questions using the worksheets, encourage groups to record questions that they have difficulty answering on the back of the worksheet. Tell them that they will have an opportunity to discuss these questions at the end of the game. Then, after the pie board has been filled, ask for volunteers from different teams to identify questions that their teams could not answer. Discuss as a whole group.

3. Ask the teams to think of questions that they would include in this game if they were using it to teach colleagues about HIV.

HIVial PURSUIT: ANSWER SHEET

Epidemiology	*Transmission*
1. _____	1. _____
2. _____	2. _____
3. _____	3. _____

Immunization	*Testing*
1. _____	1. _____
2. _____	2. _____
3. _____	3. _____

Prevention	*Research and Treatment*
1. _____	1. _____
2. _____	2. _____
3. _____	3. _____

Legal Issues

1. _____

2. _____

3. _____

HIVIAL PURSUIT: GAME QUESTIONS

Epidemiology

1. What are three risk factors for pediatric HIV infection?

2. Name three exposure categories reported in cases of adults and adolescents with AIDS.

3. What transmission category now accounts for 23% of all AIDS cases in the United States?

Optional Question

1. In the United States, women and children with AIDS are primarily from which ethnic groups?

Transmission

1. Regarding HIV transmission, which is the riskiest of unsafe sex acts?

2. What is the percentage of risk of an HIV-infected woman transmitting HIV to her infant before or at the time of delivery?

3. Who poses a higher risk of infecting other children within a classroom setting? (a) a child with HIV   (b) a child with measles   (c) a child who is a carrier of hepatitis

Optional Questions

1. Name three agents capable of inactivating HIV.

2. Transmission of HIV has been documented to have occurred through which body fluids?

Immune System

1. What specific part(s) of the body's protective mechanism does the HIV virus attack and what does this cause?

2. HIV causes an individual to be susceptible to what diseases (problems)? Name at least two.

Testing

1. What two steps are being followed to protect the blood supply from HIV contamination (blood being collected from an infected donor)?

2. With regard to testing or screening for HIV, what does the "window" mean?

3. What specifically is being measured when HIV screening is done?

Prevention

1. Name two ways that educators and medical professionals can prevent the transmission of HIV infection in their work.

2. Name two ways for everyone to prevent the transmission or spread of HIV infection.

3. What three details about condoms and their use are very important regarding the prevention and spread of HIV?

Research and Treatment

1. Name one medication (prophylaxis) used to prevent PCP in children and adults with HIV infection.

2. Name two antiviral–antiretroviral medications used to treat or used in the course of HIV infection.

Legal Issues

1. What is required for a health care provider to share an individual's HIV status with other providers?

2. What legal protection against discrimination exists for a person with HIV infection?

HIV_{IAL} PURSUIT: GAME ANSWERS

Epidemiology

1. What are three risk factors for pediatric HIV infection? *Ans.* Mother who is HIV positive; parents who are HIV drug users; sexual abuse; hemophilia; transfusion prior to 1985.

2. Name three exposure categories reported in cases of adults and adolescents with AIDS. *Ans.* Men who have sex with men. Injection drug use (sharing needles); heterosexual contact with a partner with/or at high risk for HIV infection, hemophilia or bleeding disorder, recipient of blood.

3. What transmission category now accounts for 23% of all AIDS cases in the United States? *Ans.* Injecting drug use

Optional Question

1. In the United States, women and children with AIDS are primarily from which ethnic groups? *Ans.* African-American and Hispanic

---

Transmission

1. Regarding HIV transmission, which is the riskiest of unsafe sex acts? *Ans.* Unprotected anal sex

2. What is the percentage of risk of an HIV-infected woman transmitting HIV to her infant before or at the time of delivery? *Ans.* Approximately 30%

3. Who poses a higher risk of infecting other children within a classroom setting? (a) a child with HIV   (b) a child with measles   (c) a child who is a carrier of hepatitis   *Ans.* (b) a child with measles

Optional Questions

1. Name three agents capable of inactivating HIV. *Ans.* Soap and water; bleach, 10% solution; 70% alcohol; Lysol II; hydrogen peroxide, and others

2. Transmission of HIV has been documented to have occurred through which body fluids? *Ans.* Semen, vaginal secretions, blood, breast milk

---

Immune System

1. What specific part(s) of the body's protective mechanism does the HIV virus attack and what does this cause? *Ans.* The T-cells, the lymphocytes; cellular immunity; and this causes the person to be susceptible to infections, opportunistic infections, and cancers

2. HIV causes an individual to be susceptible to what diseases (problems)? Name at least two. *Ans.* Opportunistic diseases; PCP; infections, viral, fungus; thrush; cancers, Kaposi's sarcoma; dementia; diarrhea; wasting; malnutrition; and others

Testing

1. What two steps are being followed to protect the blood supply from HIV contamination (blood being collected from an infected donor)? *Ans.* Screening (questionnaire about risk factors) and all blood from donors is being tested for HIV

2. With regard to testing or screening for HIV, what does the "window" mean? *Ans.* Time between when the person comes in contact (becomes infected with HIV) and when his or her body makes the substance (antibody) that can be measured on a test

3. What specifically is being measured when HIV screening is done? *Ans.* Antibody

Prevention

1. Name two ways that educators and medical professionals can prevent the transmission of HIV infection in their work. *Ans.* Follow universal precautions and handwashing

2. Name two ways for everyone to prevent the transmission or spread of HIV infection. *Ans.* Do not use IV drugs; practice safe sex; mutual monogamy

3. What three details about condoms and their use are very important regarding the prevention and spread of HIV? *Ans.* (1) Made of latex; (2) use from beginning (at erection); (3) use with spermicide that kills HIV (non-oxynol 9 is one). Extra answer: do not use oil-based lubricants.

Research and Treatment

1. Name one medication (prophylaxis) used to prevent PCP in children and adults with HIV infection. *Ans.* Bactrim; Septra; pentamidine, dapsone

2. Name two antiviral–antiretroviral medications used to treat or used in the course of HIV infection. *Ans.* AZT (azidothyamine); Retrovir (zidovudine); ddI; ddC; acyclovir; Gancyclovir

Legal Issues

1. What is required for a health care provider to share an individual's HIV status with other providers? *Ans.* Informed consent

2. What legal protection against discrimination exists for a person with HIV infection? *Ans.* Americans with Disabilities Act, Section 504 of the Rehabilitation Act of 1973, Constitution, Equal Protection Clause 14th Amendement (cannot withhold benefits accessible to other citizens)

DO, DEFER, DELEGATE, DUMP!
A TIME MANAGEMENT ACTIVITY

Frederick Vertrees

Fred Vertrees *is an instructional designer and training consultant in the Human Resource Division of American Airlines at its headquarters in Fort Worth, Texas (MD 5110, 4333 Amon Carter Blvd., 76155, 817-963-6913). He has given presentations at both the North American Simulation and Gaming Association (NASAGA) and the International Simulation and Gaming Association (ISAGA) conference. He is also a member of NSPI. Fred would like to thank his colleague, Laurie Fry, for her help and motivation on this project.*

Overview Have you ever walked into your office on a Monday morning and felt completely overwhelmed by the work that sits on your desk? This time management activity begins with the Monday morning scenario and then challenges participants to prioritize their own workload into four distinct categories: *do, defer, delegate,* and *dump.*

Suggested Time 45 minutes

Materials Needed
✓ Form A (Participant Instructions)
✓ Form B (Do, Defer, Delegate, Dump Example)
✓ 20 items from each participant's desk or in-basket
✓ Two sets of additional in-basket items (40 pieces total). *These could include a variety of memos, electronic mail messages, Post-it™ notes, phone messages, receipts for business expenses, performance appraisals, or other human resource documentation.*

Procedure
1. Begin by asking the group to define the terms "do," "defer," "delegate," and "dump." Write the group's responses on flip chart paper in the front of the room where everyone can see it. Encourage discussion as to what each of these terms means in the work environment that they face everyday.

2. Ask the participants to take out the 20 items that they brought to the training session. If one or more participants forgot to bring their own items, supply them with the generic in-basket. Ask the participants to

assign a number to each item in front of them from 1 to 20. (*Note:* Remind the participants that they are not to prioritize or separate out these items yet.)

3. Distribute Form A and Form B to each participant. Review the directions found on Form A.

4. Ask the group to visualize themselves facing their desks at 8 A.M. on a typical Monday morning. Using Form A, ask the participants to separate each of their in-basket items into one of the four categories shown on the form. Review the example shown on Form B. Refer back to the group's flip-charted definitions for each term found on Form A.

5. After the participants have completed Form A individually (approximately 5 minutes), ask them to find a partner with whom they would not mind sharing the contents of their in-basket. One participant reveals how the work was distributed as the listener takes notes and asks prompting questions as to how decisions were made. Ask the participants to switch roles after approximately 10 minutes of discussion.

6. Reconvene the whole group and ask the participants to share the time management strategies that they learned as a part of this exercise. How do they set priorities on a daily, weekly or monthly basis? How do they handle the number of incoming phone calls, electronic mail messages, and voice mail messages that they receive? What are some of their best strategies for managing the flow of paper that crosses their desks?

7. *Optional:* Deliver a brief lecture on proven time management techniques as a follow-up to the group discussion.

Take a careful look at the items in front of you. What must you take care of right now? What can you do at a later time? What might be appropriate for someone else to handle? What deserves to go in the trash? Write the number that you have assigned to each item in your in-basket under the appropriate category. Each of the 20 items must go into one and only one of the four categories. Try to distribute your decisions evenly.

Do

Defer

Delegate

Dump

Do
1, 7, 9,
15, 17

Defer
6, 10, 11,
18, 19

Delegate
2, 3, 8,
12, 16

Dump
4, 5, 13,
14, 20

GIVING "I MESSAGES": SKILL PRACTICE AND DISCUSSION*

Kimberly Stott

Kimberly E. Stott *is the national director of training and development for Devereux, 19 S. Waterloo Road, Devon, Pennsylvania, 19333, 610-964-3043. Devereux is the nation's largest nonprofit provider of services to people with mental health and developmental disabilities. Kimberly specializes in the design and delivery of management training and professional development programs. She has extensive experience as an educator, counselor, and advocate for individuals victimized by domestic violence and child abuse.*

Overview   This activity gives participants the opportunity to practice formulating effective and assertive statements to be used in resolving conflict. The specific skill that is learned is how to compose "I messages." A "you message" blames or attacks the other person. An "I message" gives the receiver feedback about his or her behavior. When used in conflict situations, "I messages" impress on another person your needs and concerns without making him or her unduly defensive.

Suggested Time   40 minutes

Materials Needed   ✓ Form A ("I Message" Worksheet)
✓ Form B (Answer Key to "I Message" Worksheet)

Procedure   1. Explain what an "I message" is and how it works. Make these key points:

   • An "I message" communicates how you experience another person's behavior.

   • An "I message" is feedback, rather than criticism. It lets another person learn how his or her behavior feels to you and how it affects you.

*This activity is based on "Practicing Confrontive I Messages" in *Effectiveness Training for Personal and Professional Development*, by Linda Adams, Solana Beach, CA: Effectiveness Training, Inc., 1987.

- An "I message" is usually experienced by the receiver as a positive attempt to communicate one's needs and concerns. Therefore, the other person is more likely to respond to these needs and concerns than if he or she were coerced to do so.

2. Distribute Form A to participants.

3. Review the directions and example with participants.

4. Ask participants to read each situation and formulate a description of the behavior, feelings, and effects on me, and an "I Message" statement for each. (Allow 10 minutes for completion of this section.)

5. After 10 minutes, distribute Form B. Ask participants to compare their responses on Form A to those found on Form B.

6. Obtain participants' views about "I Messages." Ask the following questions:

- Do they feel comfortable or awkward?

- How do you feel other people will react when you express "I messages" in conflict situations?

- When would they work? When would they not work?

Listen to these views and reflect what you hear. Model active listening.

7. Obtain real-life conflict situations that participants have experienced. Invite participants to role play by giving "I Messages" in those situations. Provide as much skill practice as possible.

8. Once again, obtain participants' reactions to "I Messages." Urge them to experiment with using "I Messages." Explain that the only way to accurately assess their impact is to try using them.

"I MESSAGE" WORKSHEET

Directions: Read each situation and the accompanying "You Message." Then fill in the three columns.

1. Describe the behavior that you find unacceptable.
2. Describe the feelings you have about the behavior.
3. Describe how the behavior affects you in any tangible way.

Next, compose an "I Message" using the three descriptions.

Example: A colleague continuously interrupts you, especially in meetings or in other public settings. Up to now, you have silently endured it. "You Message": "You are so rude I can't believe it!"

"I Message" Formula

Description of Behavior	Feelings	Effects on Me
Interrupting when I'm talking	Hurt, frustrated, put down, embarrassed	Can't say what I want

I Message: "I get frustrated when you interrupt me because I can't finish what I want to say."

Situation 1: Each time you ask your supervisor for information related to a key project that you are working on, he or she keeps you waiting for a reply. You have ignored it and laughed about it, but no longer.

You Message: "You never get back to me with the information I need to get my job done."

"I Message" Formula

Description of Behavior	Feelings	Effects on Me

I Message:

Situation 2: Your new employee failed to deliver a priority package that needed to leave your office yesterday. He never mentioned anything to you about the omission and has made no effort to mail the package this morning.

You Message: "You are so incompetent I can't believe it!"

"I Message" Formula

Description of Behavior	Feelings	Effects on Me

I Message:

_____

Situation 3: You are the supervisor of a small department. A couple of your employees have been coming in late off and on for about two weeks.

You Message: "If you don't stop coming in late, you're going to get fired."

"I Message" Formula

Description of Behavior	Feelings	Effects on Me

I Message:

_____

Situation 4: You are trying to conduct a meeting with several colleagues; however, several other co-workers are talking loudly in the next room, making it impossible for you to hear one another speak.

You Message: "You are making too much noise; keep it down!"

"I Message" Formula

Description of Behavior	Feelings	Effects on Me

I Message:

_____

Situation 1: Each time you ask your supervisor for information related to a key project that you are working on, he or she keeps you waiting for a reply. You have ignored it and laughed about it, but no longer.

You Message: "You never get back to me with the information I need to get my job done."

"I Message" Formula

Description of Behavior	Feelings	Effects on Me
Delays providing necessary information	Frustrated and angry	Can't get job done

I Message: "I feel frustrated when you don't provide me with the information I need to complete this project."

Situation 2: Your new employee failed to deliver a priority package that needed to leave your office yesterday. He never mentioned anything to you about the omission and has made no effort to mail the package this morning.

You Message: "You are so incompetent I can't believe it!"

"I Message" Formula

Description of Behavior	Feelings	Effects on Me
Did not mail priority package	Angry, disappointed, frustrated	Missed deadline

I Message: "I am very angry that you did not mail this priority package, which has caused us to miss a crucial deadline."

Situation 3: You are the supervisor of a small department. A couple of your employees have been coming in late off and on for about two weeks.

You Message: "If you don't stop coming in late, you're going to get fired."

"I Message" Formula

Description of Behavior	Feelings	Effects on Me
Repeated lateness	Concerned, frustrated	Reduced productivity

I Message: "Your repeated lateness is causing me concern. I am particularly worried about the impact on our productivity."

Situation 4: You are trying to conduct a meeting with several colleagues; however, several other co-workers are talking loudly in the next room, making it impossible for you to hear one another speak.

You Message: "You are making too much noise; keep it down!"

"I Message" Formula

Description of Behavior	Feelings	Effects on Me
Loud talking, noise	Annoyed, angry, frustrated	Cannot hear one another; cannot conduct meeting effectively

I Message: "I'm having a difficult time hearing my colleagues due to the noise in the hall, and I'm getting frustrated with all the interruptions."

DIVERSITY: LESSONS WITH COLORED MARKERS

13

Michael Tindal

Michael Tindal *is a team leader for claims at Progressive Insurance Company, 41 Leopard Road, Paoli, PA 19301, 610-644-7700. Mike is a former claims trainer and is currently enrolled in the Graduate School of Education at Temple University, pursuing a master's degree in psychoeducational processes. He is also a member of Mensa and ranks fourth kyu in the martial art of Aikido.*

Overview   This series of activities uses the metaphor of marking pens to demonstrate some important lessons about color preferences and other forms of racial bias.

Suggested Time   40 minutes

Materials Needed   ✓ Several marking pens varying in color
✓ Form A (Scoring Directions for Judges)

Procedure
1. Divide participants into as many groups as you wish as long as you have one marking pen of the same color for each member of one group and different colors for different groups. Give each group its markers of the same color. For example, a group of 4 participants might each receive a red marker, while another group might receive blue markers.

2. Ask each group to list on flip chart paper the virtues of its color. For example, red can be extolled as the color of passion, peppermint candy, and fast-food signs.

3. Allow time for participants to read the lists of other groups.

4. Change the color assigned to each group. Ask the groups to list the positive attributes of their new colors. Allow them to "borrow" attributes already listed by the group that previously had the same color.

5. If you have three or more groups, switch colors one more time and again request a new list.

6. Ask participants how the exercise affected them. Find out if participants went from a decided color preference to an acceptance of different colors. Explore the benefits of a technicolor world. Do different groups of people provide different perspectives on the world and, if so, how is that beneficial to them and their organizations?

7. Next, choose one person from each group to be a judge. Give the judges a copy of Form A. Send them outside the room.

8. Distribute to each group a set of five marking pens containing one of each of the following colors: purple, green, red, black, and blue. (You may use other colors if you cannot obtain these five.) Ask each group to create a creative *group symbol* or drawing that represents the group, such as an animal, a type of car, or an icon.

9. Have the judges return and give their respective groups a *creativity score. (Make sure the judges do not reveal the scoring criteria.)* Display the drawings and find out the score received by each group. Obtain reactions from groups about the scores that they obtained. Be unsympathetic to participants' objections to the scoring. Then disclose the scoring system.

10. Ask the participants to draw an analogy between the exercise and bias in real life. Point out that you were trying to demonstrate the capricious and illogical nature of bias based on color. Discuss whether the color of someone's skin, taken alone, affects how people react.

Directions: When you return to the room and are presented with the creative drawing of your group, look it over very carefully as if you are seriously judging its quality.

However, use this time to decide which color was used the most in the drawing.

Give 50 points if the use of the color purple dominates.
Give 40 points if the use of the color green dominates.
Give 30 points if the use of the color red dominates.
Give 20 points if the use of the color black dominates.
Give 10 points if the use of the color blue dominates.

If in doubt, use your best judgment.

Score   _____

You may refer to this sheet as you deliberate, but do not show the sheet to anyone else and do not reveal its contents.

Announce the score only to the group. If you are asked what influenced your score, tell them that you had clear criteria for judging the drawing, but you cannot reveal these criteria to them at this time.

ATTENTION! A LEARNING ASSESSMENT ACTIVITY*

Linda Roth and Laura Bierema

Linda M. Roth, *Ph.D., is an assistant professor of family medicine at Wayne State University (4201 St. Antoine, UHC 4-J, Detroit, MI 48201, 313-577-1420, LROTH@cms.cc.wayne.edu). Linda assists family medicine faculty to improve their teaching skills and consults with other faculty groups about teaching and learning strategies.* **Laura B. Bierema,** *Ed.D., is a faculty member at Washtenaw Community College (4800 E. Huron River Dr., PO Box D-1, Ann Arbor, MI 48106, 313-973-1371). Laura has a joint appointment in the Business Department and the Institute for Workforce Development, through which she develops and presents training in The Learning Organization in conjunction with the Ford Motor Company.*

Overview A glazed look creeps into several participants' eyes. You see one person yawning, followed by two more. A quick look down at a participant's notebook reveals extensive doodling. It's time to check in on learner concentration levels before the participants completely check out on you.

Attention! *A Learning Assessment Activity* focuses you and your participants on factors that contribute to or detract from learning. At a point mid-session, or perhaps just before a break, challenge learners to answer and then discuss the questions on Form A as an on-the-spot tool for assessing participant concentration. The form can be then be used as a learning barometer at several points throughout a multisession course, or you can compare participant ratings across training sessions to gain insights into overall learning patterns.

Suggested Time Variable. In long-term training sessions, invest 15 to 20 minutes for the first use of the instrument and 5 to 15 minutes for subsequent uses. In a half-day or full day, ask participants to focus on one or two of the scales only (either your choice or theirs) and take only 5 to 10 minutes.

Materials Needed Form A (Learning Self-Assessment)

*Based on "Punctuated Lectures," in *Classroom Assessment Techniques: A Handbook for College Teachers,* 2nd ed., by T. A. Angelo and K. P. Cross, 1993, San Francisco: Jossey-Bass, pp. 303–6.

Procedure   1. At the time you have chosen for the intervention, stop your current instruction. Explain to the participants that you are going to help them to focus on the role that they themselves have been playing in the learning process thus far in the session. In doing a self-assessment, they will have a chance to think about factors that contribute to or interfere with learning.

2. Distribute Form A. Ask participants to rate themselves in four categories: importance, previous knowledge and connections, concentration, and processing. Explain that they should answer the questions on the right-hand side of the form that are related to each of these topics (5 minutes).

3. Ask participants to discuss their answers with a partner (5 minutes).

4. Ask volunteers to share with the group an insight that they have had or an idea that they have learned about learning strategies. Reinforce helpful insights and productive ideas about learning strategies. Address successful techniques for both (a) increasing learning effectiveness and (b) overcoming barriers to learning (5 to 10 minutes).

5. Wrap up the discussion by encouraging participants to work at making a habit of tuning into their learning both in training and on the job. Ask them to try to understand their learning patterns—what enhances or interferes with learning from opportunities that present themselves. Help learners to understand that they (not just the instructor!) are responsible for their learning and that being a good learner leads to improved work performance. Tie principles that have arisen in the discussion to workplace issues such as collaborative problem solving with colleagues.

Variations   1. Inform participants that they can use Form A to investigate their learning strategies in other settings, such as when they are reading to learn.

2. Use the form to assess how the group as a whole is concentrating, and have learners answer questions such as "How can I help others to be focused?" and "What do I need from others to focus myself?"

Importance	How **important** is this information to me? Slightly————Very 1 2 3 4 5	If the information is important, why? If the information does not seem important to me, how can I look at it differently to find a way to use it for myself and/or others?
Previous knowledge and connections	How much did I **know** about this topic before the session? Little————Much 1 2 3 4 5	Is a lack of knowledge or preparation preventing me from learning? If so, what can I do about this today? If I know something about this topic, how can I connect today's new information to what I already know?
Concentration	How well am I **concentrating** during this session? Poorly————Well 1 2 3 4 5	If I've stayed focused, what has helped? If I've been distracted, why? How can I refocus?
Processing	How well am I **understanding** the material? Slightly————Deeply 1 2 3 4 5	If I'm understanding deeply, what is contributing to my understanding? If I'm not understanding deeply, what seems to be interfering with my comprehension? What steps can I take to improve my understanding?

ASSESSMENT INSTRUMENTS

In this section of *The 1996 McGraw-Hill Training and Performance Sourcebook*, you will find six assessment instruments. With these instruments, you will be able to assess:

✓ Issues related to the design, delivery, and results of training.
✓ Question asking.
✓ Electronic performance support systems.
✓ Computer literacy.

The instruments are designed both to evaluate training/performance issues and to suggest areas for improvement. Most are not for research purposes. Instead, they are intended to build awareness, provide feedback about your own specific situation, and promote group reflection.

In selecting instruments for publication, a premium was placed on questionnaires or survey forms that are easy to understand and quick to complete. Preceding each instrument is an overview that contains the key questions to be assessed. The instrument itself is on a separate page(s) to make reproduction more convenient. All of the instruments are scorable and contain guidelines for scoring interpretation. Some include questions for followup discussion.

Many of these instruments are ideal to utilize as activities in training sessions. Participants can complete the instrument you have selected prior to or during the session. After completion, ask participants to score and interpret their own results. Then, have them compare outcomes with other participants, either in pairs or in larger groupings. Be careful, however, to stress that the data from these instruments are not "hard." They *suggest* rather than *demonstrate* facts about people or situations. Ask participants to compare scores to their own perceptions. If they do not match, urge them to consider why. In some cases, the discrepancy may be due to the crudeness of the measurement device. In others, the discrepancy may result from distorted self-perceptions. Urge participants to open themselves to new feedback and awareness.

Other instruments will help you and others to assess future training needs. Again, it would be useful to show and discuss the data that emerges with others involved in the area under evaluation.

You may also wish to use some instruments as a basis for planning retreats or staff meetings. Have participants complete the instruments prior to the session. Then, summarize the results and open it up to team discussion.

If you choose this option, be sure to state the process clearly to respondents. You might want to use the following text:

We are planning to get together soon to identify issues that need to be worked through in order to maximize our future effectivenss. An excellent way to begin doing some of this work is to collect information through a questionnaire and to feed back that information for group discussion.

I would like you to join with your colleagues in filling out the attached questionnaire. Your honest responses will enable us to have a clear, objective view of our situation.

Your participation will be totally anonymous. My job will be to summarize the results and report them to the group for reaction.

You can also share the instruments with others in your organization who might find them useful for their own purposes. In some cases, merely reading through the questions is a valuable exercise in self and group reflection.

HOW EFFECTIVE IS YOUR TRAINING STYLE?

15

Jean Barbazette

Jean Barbazette *is the president of The Training Clinic (645 Seabreeze Drive, Seal Beach, CA, 90740, 310-430-2484), a training consulting firm she founded in 1977. Her company conducts needs assessments, designs training programs and specializes in new employee orientation, train-the-trainer, and enhancing the quality of training and instruction for major national and international clients. She is the author of* **Successful New Employee Orientation** *(Pfeiffer & Company, 1994).*

OVERVIEW

This assessment instrument, the *Trainer Style Inventory,* assists in identifying the effectiveness of a trainer's current instructional style. Trainers are most effective when they help learners progress through the five sequential steps in the adult learning process. Different skills are helpful at each step of the process. This inventory measures the trainer's preferences for using all these skills and summarizes the results into four styles.

Trainers, classroom instructors, adult educators, and those who conduct on-the-job training can all use the *Trainer Style Inventory* to identify style preference(s) and a range of styles. Since a different style is best matched with each of the five adult learning steps, a range of all four styles is ideal. Trainers are encouraged to consider when each style is appropriately used, the advantages of their dominant style, the disadvantages of the overuse of a preferred style, and the disadvantages of not using a least preferred style. Inventory results can also facilitate the development of a personal performance plan to gain greater comfort with each of the four different styles.

The *Trainer Styles Inventory* matches training styles to the five sequential steps of adult learning. These steps are as follows:

Adult Learning Steps

1. *Trainer setup:* For a learning activity to be successful, it must be set up appropriately by the trainer so that participants understand

what they are going to do and why they are doing it. Adult learners become motivated when they understand the benefit or importance of the activity to themselves. Directions and ground rules are usually included regarding how the learning activity is to be conducted. Setup can include the following:

- ✓ Telling participants the purpose of the activity
- ✓ Dividing participants into groups
- ✓ Assigning roles
- ✓ Giving ground rules
- ✓ Explaining what the participants are going to do
- ✓ Telling participants why they are doing the activity without giving away what is to be discovered

2. *Participant activity:* Engaging activities that put a premium on involvement increase the likelihood that adult learners will absorb their content. Activities that appeal to the senses of sight, hearing, and touch are additionally involving. The second step in the adult learning cycle includes such activities as the following:

- ✓ Session starters
- ✓ Lectures
- ✓ Case studies
- ✓ Role plays
- ✓ Questionnaires
- ✓ Simulation or instructional games
- ✓ Inventories

3. *Learner reaction:* This step is essential to help to conclude the activity and assist learners in identifying what happened during the activity. Learners share their reactions by analyzing what happened to themselves and other participants, how their behavior affected others, and the like. Common questions that trainers ask are "What was your partner's reaction when you did ...?" or "What helped or hindered your progress?" Trainers may also ask participants to summarize the key points from the lecture, role play, or case study. Sometimes it is appropriate to have each participant write down his or her reactions so that they are not influenced by another person before sharing them.

    Sharing a reaction is the beginning step of developing a pattern. If some participants do not share their reactions, it is difficult to end the activity, and they may prolong some unfinished business that spills over into other activities during the workshop.

4. *Concept identification:* This is the "so what did I learn?" step. Questions that encourage reflection include "What did you learn about how to conduct an interview, discipline a subordinate, or teach a new job?" If this step is left out, learning will be incomplete.

Participants will have been entertained, but may not be able to apply new learning to similar situations outside the classroom. When concepts are inferred from an activity, adult learners are ready to apply these newly learned or recently confirmed concepts to future situations.

5. *Learner application:* This is the "so what now?" step. Adult learners are asked to use and apply the new information learned from the activity and confirmed through a discussion of general concepts to their situation. This often involves an action step like "How will you use this questioning technique the next time a subordinate asks you for a favor?" or "In what situations would you be more effective if you used this technique?" If this step is left out, the learner may not see the relationship between the learning activity and his or her job or situation and consider what was learned by others as not useful to him or her.

TRAINER STYLE INVENTORY*

Directions: For each of the twelve sets of items, rank your preferred training style from 1 to 4 in each set. A ranking of 1 is your *most preferred* or *most often used* training style, 2 is your next preferred style or method, and 4 is your *least preferred* or *least used method* or style of training. If you are having a difficult time deciding, rate the type of activity you like best as 1.

1. a. _____ use small-group discussion
   b. _____ give a lecture
   c. _____ provide self-paced reading material
   d. _____ combine a lecture with large-group discussion

2. a. _____ conduct a demonstration
   b. _____ use exercises or puzzles to teach a point
   c. _____ assist or coach a learner one on one
   d. _____ use audio recordings or music to enhance learning

3. a. _____ use tools or a symbolic demonstration to present an idea
   b. _____ guide learners as they practice a skill or act out a role play
   c. _____ provide expert guest speakers for learners to listen to
   d. _____ give directions to complete a task

4. a. _____ conduct a structured small-group discussion
   b. _____ allow learners to question and discuss at anytime during training
   c. _____ limit learner participation
   d. _____ structure quiet time to reflect as part of the learning process

5. a. _____ give immediate individual feedback to evaluate learning
   b. _____ measure learning using specific, objective criteria
   c. _____ measure learning subjectively, either verbally or in writing
   d. _____ help learners to reflect on and evaluate their own progress

6. a. _____ be recognized as a practical expert on the subject
   b. _____ have an academic reputation or be a published author on a subject
   c. _____ be seen as a coach, mentor, or advisor to the learner
   d. _____ be seen as an equal, peer, or friend of the learner

*Special thanks to Linda Ernst and Melissa Smith, who helped refine and edit the inventory.

7. a. _____ help learners to develop an understanding of theory

   b. _____ teach useful skills

   c. _____ help learners to apply learning to their situations

   d. _____ instruct learners on new ways of doing things

8. a. _____ offer observations and suggestions to learners

   b. _____ listen to learners' concerns

   c. _____ direct the learning experience

   d. _____ help learners to understand the learning experience

9. a. _____ see that everyone is involved

   b. _____ explain how something works

   c. _____ help learners to determine causes through reason

   d. _____ ask questions to help discovery learning

10. a. _____ help learners to share and interpret reactions from a learning experience

   b. _____ extract general concepts from a learning experience

   c. _____ direct a learning activity

   d. _____ encourage learners to plan and verbalize how new learning will be used

11. a. _____ lead learners to share a common understanding

   b. _____ let learners draw their own conclusions

   c. _____ allow learners to enjoy the learning experience

   d. _____ get learners to evaluate learning with objective criteria

12. a. _____ learning occurs when trainees have adequate resources and problem-solving skills

   b. _____ learning is a shared responsibility between trainer and trainee

   c. _____ the trainer is responsible to make sure that learning takes place

   d. _____ learning occurs when a trainer provides a strong theoretical, factual base for an independent-thinking learner

SCORING THE TRAINER STYLE INVENTORY

Directions: Record the points from each line in the correct column. Total the number of points in each column. Each column represents a style.

Instructor	Explorer	Thinker	Guide
1b ____	1a ____	1c ____	1d ____
2a ____	2d ____	2b ____	2c ____
3d ____	3c ____	3a ____	3b ____
4c ____	4b ____	4d ____	4a ____
5b ____	5a ____	5c ____	5d ____
6a ____	6d ____	6b ____	6c ____
7d ____	7c ____	7a ____	7b ____
8c ____	8b ____	8d ____	8a ____
9b ____	9a ____	9c ____	9d ____
10c ____	10a ____	10b ____	10d ____
11d ____	11c ____	11a ____	11b ____
12c ____	12b ____	12d ____	12a ____

If the total of all four columns doesn't add up to 120, check your math.

TRAINER STYLES INTERPRETATION

The score with the *lowest* number is your *most* preferred or most often used style. The *highest* score is your *least* used or preferred style. A difference of more than 8 points between the highest and lowest scores indicates a lack of flexibility in using your least preferred style. Scores within 4 points of each other indicate flexibility in using different styles. Transfer your scores from the previous page to each training style given next.

Instructor Score: _____

The **Instructor** enjoys setting up and directing the learning activity (steps 1 and 2 in the Adult Learning Steps). The Instructor is most comfortable giving directions and taking charge of the learning activity. The Instructor prefers to tell the learners what to do, is well organized and self-confident, and concentrates on one item at a time. The Instructor provides examples, controls learner participation, and uses lectures effectively.

Explorer Score: _____

The **Explorer** is most comfortable helping learners to share and interpret their reactions to a learning activity (step 3 in the Adult Learning Steps). The Explorer is a good listener who creates an open learning environment, encourages free expression, and assures that everyone is involved in the discussion. The Explorer is alert to nonverbal cues and shows empathy for the feelings and emotions of the learners. The Explorer appears relaxed and unhurried. The Explorer is accepting of the learner's reactions and encourages self-directed learning.

Thinker Score: _____

The **Thinker** is most comfortable helping the learner generalize concepts from the reactions to a learning experience (step 4 in the Adult Learning Steps). The Thinker helps learners to categorize, organize, and integrate their reactions into theories, principles, and generalizations. The Thinker focuses on ideas and thoughts, rather than feelings and emotions. The Thinker acknowledges different interpretations and theories. Independent thinking is encouraged based on objective information. The Thinker assists learners in making connections between the past and the present. The Thinker is often a practiced observer of the learning activity.

Guide Score: _____

The **Guide** is most comfortable helping learners to apply how to use new learning in their own situations (step 5 in the Adult Learning Steps). The Guide prefers to involve trainees in activities, problem solving, discussions, and evaluations of their own progress. Experimentation with practical application is encouraged. The Guide encourages trainees to draw on each other and the trainer as resources. The Guide acts as a facilitator to translate theory into practical action. The Guide focuses on meaningful and applicable solutions to real-life problems and encourages active participation.

USING YOUR TRAINER STYLE

The following are suggestions for when to use each style and some of the advantages and disadvantages of each style. A disadvantage can come from overuse of a dominant (most preferred) style or underuse of a least preferred style.

Instructor

When: The Instructor style is best used to complete adult learning steps 1 and 2: set up and conduct the learning activity.

Advantages: Many subject matter experts prefer the Instructor style. They are quite comfortable in their expertise and easily and willingly offer their knowledge and experience to the learner. Many adults learn information when presented in a clear and concise manner by an expert Instructor. Instructors are clear about setting the ground rules for an activity, which brings clarity to their directions.

Disadvantages (overuse): If the Instructor ignores the experience of the learner or spends too much effort controlling the learning situation, adults could be discouraged from participating. Many adults do not learn well by just listening to the expert who overuses the lecture method.

Disadvantages (underuse): The trainer who does not like to use the Instructor style and feels it is too controlling may have difficulty handling the class. This can result in unclear directions for an activity or ambiguous ground rules. When participants are unsure, they sometimes need firm direction in order for learning to take place. A brief lecture often helps provide a firm foundation for later learning activities, especially when the adult learners have no experience in the subject being learned.

Explorer

When: The Explorer style is best used to complete adult learning step 3: share and interpret reactions.

Advantages: Most trainers with good interpersonal skills will feel comfortable using the Explorer style. Adult learners seem to flourish when given the opportunity to express opinions and reactions. They feel valued when their experiences are validated. This style maintains a positive learning climate.

Disadvantages (overuse): Not all participants are interested in sharing their feelings or reactions to a learning experience. Some participants can easily move through this step with little assistance with a brief recognition of what took place during a learning activity. Overuse of this style can be seen as intrusive by the participants and may result in frustrating the learner who seeks a faster pace.

Disadvantages (underuse): Unless participants have a chance to reflect on what happened in the learning activity, it will be difficult to determine what larger concepts could be learned. Ignoring this step or telling the participants what happened or was supposed to happen in the learning activity usually results in frustration for the adult learner. Learning takes place for the adults when they can reflect on their own experiences.

Thinker

When: The Thinker style is best used to complete adult learning step 4: identify concepts from learner reactions.

Advantages: Abstract thinkers are most comfortable with the trainer who uses the Thinker style. A discussion of ideas is great fun and mental exercise for some adult learners. Adults also like having their personal experiences and reflections elevated to concepts.

Disadvantages (overuse): Learners who are not comfortable with abstract ideas sometimes have difficulty with this style of training. The concrete or practical learner can become impatient and want to move more quickly to get to how the ideas can be used.

Disadvantages (underuse): Learners who are not exposed to taking individual, concrete experiences and translating them into generalizations or concepts usually have difficulty applying new experiences to their own situation. Some learners may also have difficulty applying what is learned in one situation to other similar situations if this step is missed.

Guide

When: The Guide style is best used to complete adult learning step 5: apply concepts to the learner's situation.

Advantages: The Guide style is very effective with practical learners. Linking training concepts to a learner's situation is a strong motivator for learning. It is a particularly effective style when conducting on-the-job training. The trainer who uses the Guide style encourages learners to identify a variety of ways to apply the learning points from a single activity.

Disadvantages (overuse): Guides sometimes tend to rush through the other four adult learning steps to get to the practical result or learning point.

Disadvantages (underuse): Not using the Guide style makes learning academic and less attractive to real-world learners.

Development planning: Since the ideal result of the inventory is a balance (within 8 points) of the four styles, identify whether the disadvantages here apply to your situation. Select which style(s) you want to develop and look back through the inventory to identify specific skills to develop or which skills require more practice in order to be used more comfortably.

DOES YOUR TRAINING DEPARTMENT NEED REALIGNMENT?

16

Diane Gayeski

Diane Gayeski, *Ph.D., is a partner in OmniCom Associates (407 Coddington Road, Ithaca, NY 14850, 607-272-7700, gayeski@ithaca.edu), an international consultancy that helps clients to design and apply interactive media and new performance analysis and intervention tools to organizational training and communication systems. The author of seven books, she is a frequent conference speaker and leader of workshops and executive briefings. She is also associate professor and chair of the Department of Corporate Communication at Ithaca College.*

OVERVIEW

As organizations of all types grapple with major demographic changes in the marketplace, new management theories, and emerging technologies, many companies are looking toward their training departments to transform employees' skills and attitudes. This quick checklist helps you to assess how well your training practices are aligned with your organization's change initiatives and serves as a springboard from which you can think about new processes and philosophies for organizational learning.

This assessment instrument takes about 5 minutes to complete and about 15 minutes to read and think over using the interpretation sheet. Don't read the interpretation sheet until you have completed the *Training Alignment Checklist.*

TRAINING ALIGNMENT CHECKLIST

Check each that is advocated in your organization's value statements or programs.

_____ Total quality management (TQM)

_____ Employee empowerment

_____ Teamwork

_____ Just-in-time manufacturing

_____ Diversity awareness

_____ Environmental consciousness

_____ Participatory decision making

_____ Self-managed teams

_____ Continual learning (the "learning organization")

_____ Global manufacturing and marketing

_____ Downsizing and rightsizing

_____ Management of information overload

Number of checkmarks for list 1: _____

Which of these practices occur in your organization?

_____ Employees are "sent" to courses by managers.

_____ Training is generally based on input from one or two subject matter experts.

_____ Most company news is written by communications staff.

_____ Policies and procedures are documented only in printed materials.

_____ More messages are sent from the top down than from the bottom up.

_____ Communication and training professionals are rewarded for the amount of materials or number of programs or courses that they produce.

_____ Training and documentation generally present one "best" way to approach a task.

_____ Training materials do not include or acknowledge the input of employees.

_____ Most training courses are led by one instructor.

_____ Most formal information is transmitted by print.

_____ Documentation and training cannot keep up with new product and policy introductions.

_____ Employee communications, advertising and public relations, training, information systems, and media production are all separate departments.

_____ Communication interventions are evaluated by "smile sheets," which measure how much the audience enjoyed the program or materials.

_____ Most formal meetings with management consist of announcements.

_____ Most media and courses are generated by requests from managers.

_____ Most training is done away from the actual work site.

Number of checkmarks for list 2: _____

How did you respond to the assessment? If you checked off at least several boxes on both lists 1 and 2, you probably realized that many of the practices on list 2 are actually at odds with the statements found on list 1. Often the practices of training departments actually contradict the content of what they are supposed to teach!

For example, managers "send" employees to courses on empowerment, whether or not they want to participate. Courses in diversity and teamwork are developed with the input of one subject matter expert and attempt to teach the "one right way" to do something. Trainers advocate total quality management, but assess training influence by the number of pages or hours in a course and by participants' statements of enjoyment of the course or gripes, rather than by measurable performance improvement. Although the organization might tout participatory management, most training and documentation are produced through the results of requests by managers, not by their subordinates, and these materials generally do not use (or at least acknowledge) the input of regular employees. Despite attempts to provide information faster, reduce paperwork, and simplify jobs, training and documentation are still laborious, long, paper-intensive tasks in most organizations.

Unfortunately, many training activities are sending the wrong messages to participants about what is really important in the organization. Either the value statements (like empowerment, diversity, and participatory management) are not really supported or are unattainable, or communication about these issues is at odds with the activities themselves. In many organizations, this is leading to mass confusion and skepticism—employees criticizing management for not "walking the talk" and for launching "programs of the month" without any concrete changes ever taking place.

Don't feel hopeless if you realize that your training and communication systems are not well aligned with your organization's initiatives. The practices described on list 2 have been the traditionally accepted modes of operation for many years. However, just as other areas of business are being reengineered, so too should training and development.

Think about this: training, documentation, and employee communication programs are the "voice" of that fictitious "persona" that is your organization. What do these interventions tell people about who they are and how they are valued in the organization? It is common for organizations to tell employees to "just sit tight … you don't have the capacity to share your knowledge with your colleagues, and you don't even know when you need training. We'll ask the real experts around here what you need to know, and you'll be told when and how you are to learn it." While the rest of the organization is running at 100 miles per hour, using computer models, decision-support systems, and statistical process control to deliver better products in less time, training is still grinding away with traditional design and evaluation methods and, in many cases, may be holding up major company-wide initiatives.

So what are newer alternatives to the more traditional practices?

1. Employees decide what they need to know and how they should learn it.

2. Formal training courses are an uncommon way for people to learn. Everybody is a learner and a teacher, and a good knowledge management system puts the expertise of every employee in the hands of their colleagues when and where they need it. Mentoring systems are encouraged, and different and creative approaches to problem solving are acknowledged and rewarded. Interactive information systems tailor the style and content of presentations to the individual and are accessible on an as-needed basis at the work site.

3. Most company news is generated by those who create the news. It is disseminated through traditional print vehicles, as well as electronic mail, bulletin boards, "home-grown" department videos, and the like. Information flows from the bottom up, across departments, as well as from the top down. Communication is characterized by *sharing* rather than *telling*.

4. Most organizational news, policies, and procedures are made available electronically so that they can rapidly be accessed and updated.

5. While the importance of communication and learning are recognized, the most crucial job of training and organizational communication professionals is to limit *information overload*. These professionals are evaluated and rewarded based on their demonstration that their interventions resulted in improved organizational performance, not on how much people liked their projects. Every intervention needs to show a return on investment projection before it is approved. Departments do not have training budgets or communications budgets; rather, they invest money in various learning interventions in order to improve efficiency and reduce costs. In calculating the cost of communication and training projects, the costs of the design and production plus the cost of consumption—the portion of employees' salaries spent while reading the newsletter or taking the course—are included. Communication and training professionals work together so that their messages are not redundant or contradictory and, in fact, may be converged into one organizational learning department.

Take time to reconsider the traditional ways that your training department has been doing business and become aligned with your organization's change initiatives for the future.

DO YOU ASK ENOUGH QUESTIONS?

Dorothy Leeds

Dorothy Leeds *is the author of* **Smart Questions** *(McGraw-Hill, 1987),* **PowerSpeak** *(Prentice-Hall Press, 1988), and* **Marketing Yourself** *(Harper Collins, 1991), and the creator of infotainment and show-stopping training. She is president of Organizational Technologies (800 West End Avenue, NY 10025, 212-864-2424), a communications firm training salespeople, managers, and trainers. She has also published in the* **Training and Development Journal,** **National Underwriter,** *and* **Accounting Today** *and appears regularly on "Good Morning America," "The Today Show," and CNBC.*

OVERVIEW

Knowing how to ask a smart question can get you almost anything you want, anytime. So why don't we all do it? In fact, most of us think we do. We are certain that we ask plenty of questions, particularly in those situations known to require skillful probing. The truth is that most of us make statements most of the time. Impatience, nervousness, or a need to get our point across pushes us into telling rather than asking and talking rather than listening.

The Smart Question Survey is designed to help people to change their basic communication approach and to put them in a questioning mode. The survey will work for anyone, whether his or her business is in management, sales, or customer service. The importance of asking questions is also essential to all types of training and for trainers as well.

THE SMART QUESTION SURVEY*

This survey examines if you ask enough questions when you are at work. To get the greatest benefit from this assessment, don't ponder the questions; go with your first, automatic response. Before you can make smart questions a habit, you must look at your current style. Try to imagine each situation as if it were really happening to you, then circle the answer that comes closest to your immediate response. When you have answered all the questions, add up the points and read about the implications of your score.

Circle the response that most closely represents what you would say or do in a similar situation.

1. A departmental report is criticized. You say,

    a. "I'm sorry, it's my fault."

    b. "What went wrong?"

    c. "Why does this always happen to me?"

    d. "My people never check their work."

2. Turned down for a raise, you

    a. start job hunting.

    b. ask yourself, "What's wrong with me?"

    c. ask yourself, "What can I do to get a yes?"

    d. stick with it, even though you feel demoralized and de-energized.

3. Your boss asks, "What are you doing tonight?" You answer,

    a. "I have an important appointment."

    b. "Nothing."

    c. "Why do you ask?"

    d. "I was looking forward to having some time to myself."

*This assessment instrument is excerpted from Dorothy Leeds, *Smart Questions: A New Strategy for Successful Managers.* New York: McGraw-Hill, 1987. Reprinted with permission.

4. One morning your boss gives you three top-priority projects, and then brings in a fourth. You

    a. decide to do all four to show your boss she can count on you, no matter what.

    b. accept the workload but feel furious inside because your boss has so little consideration.

    c. tell her straight out that there is no way all four jobs can be done at once.

    d. ask which of the four assignment she needs first.

5. The chairperson of a meeting of department heads says that your department should be more cooperative. You

    a. ask the chairperson for specific suggestions after the meeting.

    b. say nothing, but later complain to your associates.

    c. immediately confront the meeting chairperson and ask how you can accomplish the change.

    d. nod your head in agreement.

6. A high-level executive asks you to volunteer for a project you don't want to do. You

    a. agree reluctantly.

    b. say, "Can you tell me more about it?"

    c. refuse with a lengthy excuse.

    d. ask, "How important is this to you?"

7. You are unexpectedly asked to move to a smaller, less advantageous office. You

    a. start packing.

    b. start looking for another job.

    c. tell the office manager, "I'm on my way to a meeting, can we talk about this later?"

    d. ask your boss what's going on.

8. You schedule a meeting with a tough negotiator with whom you hope to do long-term business. To begin, you

   a. ask a direct and leading question to gain control ("What's your bottom line?")

   b. ask a nonthreatening question to establish rapport ("What do you feel is the best way to start this?")

   c. let him start off.

   d. bring along a support person to set the stage.

9. You have to make a scheduling decision that will affect your staff. You

   a. ask your boss's opinion.

   b. call a staff meeting and make a joint decision.

   c. weigh all the facts and decide for yourself.

   d. ask your staff to work it out among themselves.

10. When you are trying to show strength within a group, you usually

   a. talk louder and longer.

   b. ask probing questions.

   c. listen.

   d. come well prepared with questions and statements.

11. Your CEO has just called and given you instructions you don't understand. You

   a. take notes and hope that you will eventually be able to figure them out.

   b. ask someone else to explain the instructions.

   c. say, "I don't fully understand. Can you explain further?"

   d. ask "Can I call you back for further clarification if necessary?"

12. At an interview for a top position, the interviewer opens with "Tell me about yourself." You answer

   a. "My first job was in the mail room at ABC; after I finished college I moved up to administrative assistant. Then I was office manager for two years and then was promoted to vice-president of administrative services."

   b. "That's a difficult question; I'm not sure where to begin."

   c. "What specifically do you want to know?"

   d. "I was born in Cleveland, but my folks moved to California when I was six."

13. As a job seeker, you are told after an interview, "We'll get back to you." You

    a. ask, "When can I expect to hear from you?"

    b. smile and say thank you.

    c. ask, "When can I have an answer—I have other offers."

    d. ask, "When in the next 10 days can I call you for an answer?"

14. When someone asks your advice about a problem, you ask,

    a. "Where do you hope to end up?"

    b. "What would you like to do?"

    c. "How can I specifically help?"

    d. "Whom else have you asked for advice?"

15. An unresponsive person has been assigned to your team. You

    a. ask, "Why are you so quiet?"

    b. ask, "What do I have to do to get you to respond?"

    c. leave him alone temporarily.

    d. ask, "What projects are you working on now?"

Check through your responses and add up the number of points you received for each question.

1. a = 2   b = 5   c = 1   d = 0

Automatically accepting the blame (a) or passing the buck (d) is not a productive solution. Neither is whining (c). Obviously, asking "What went wrong?" (b) is the best approach.

2. a = 0   b = 2   c = 5   d = 0

Quitting (a) shows defensiveness and insecurity. Sticking it out (d) will serve neither yourself nor your company best. Asking, "What's wrong with me?" (b) is not the kind of self-questioning that produces results, unlike asking "What can I do to get a yes?" (c).

3. a = 2   b = 0   c = 5   d = 3

You're on the spot, because you don't know why the boss is asking. The best possible answer is (c): "Why do you ask?" It will give you all the information you need to make a choice.

4. a = 1   b = 0   c = 3   d = 5

If you knock yourself out trying to do everything (a), at least it shows that you are eager and willing. It is better than hiding your anger (b). Telling her you cannot do all the work at once (c) does not offer any solutions. But setting priorities (d) helps both of you to focus and work efficiently.

5. a = 4   b = 0   c = 5   d = 1

You have two good choices here: asking for specific suggestions after the meeting (a) is good if it is a high-level meeting; but in most situations immediately confronting the chair (c) is the best response.

6. a = 2   b = 4   c = 0   d = 5

We are all asked to do things we do not want to do. Refusing immediately (c) won't help you to get ahead; agreeing reluctantly (a) is not very good for your mental health. Asking, "How important is this to you?" (d) is best because the response may affect your decision. If it is not important, you may safely refuse; if it is very important, you may gain extra points for doing it.

7. a = 0   b = 2   c = 5   d = 3

Stall for time so that you can think about the best way to handle this (c). Don't start packing (a) or looking for a new job immediately (b), because there may be room for negotiation. Asking the boss what's going on can't hurt (d).

8. a = 2   b = 5   c = 4   d = 0

The obvious answer seems to be (a)—to gain control. But gaining control at the beginning is not always wise. The best answer is (b), to establish rapport and gain trust. The next best answer is (c), to let the other person start. If you need to bring along a support person (d), you will lose brownie points.

9. a = 1   b = 5   c = 2   d = 3

Anytime you have to make a decision involving your staff, let them participate (b). If they can solve the issue without you, by all means let them do it (d). It is all right to ask your boss's opinion, but not at the expense of involving your staff (a). In some situations, you will want to make a solo decision (c), but look for other opportunities to involve your staff.

10. a = 1   b = 4   c = 3   d = 5

Ask someone to observe you in a group and tell you honestly how you show strength. Talking louder and longer (a) does not help. Asking probing questions (b) is good, as is listening (c). But being well prepared with questions and statements (d) is the best answer, especially if it is your style to talk a lot.

11. a = 0   b = 1   c = 4   d = 5

Faking your way through (a) or asking someone else for help (b) is a dangerous route to take. Asking for immediate help (c) is not a bad response, but (d) is best. You may not need to call back, but leave yourself the opening.

12. a = 1   b = 3   c = 5   d = 0

"Tell me about yourself" is one of the most popular interview questions. The best possible answer is (c): "What specifically did you want to know?" Anything else and you are wandering off track.

13. a = 3   b = 0   c = 4   d = 5

When someone gives you a vague "We'll get back to you," smiling and saying thank you (b) is polite but ineffectual. "When can I expect to hear from you?" (a) is good, but it leaves the control in the interviewer's hands. Telling the interviewer that you have other offers may work (c) if you can be confrontational without being pushy. The best answer is "When in the next 10 days can I call for an answer?" (d), because it allows you to be proactive.

14. a = 5   b = 4   c = 4   d = 2

The best answer is (a). Before you can help someone else solve a problem, you have to know their objective. "What would you like to do?" (b) is good; it gets the person thinking for himself. "How can I specifically help?" (c) gets him to focus on what he really expects from you. "Whom else have you asked for advice?" (d) is good if you follow it with "What did they say?"

15. a = 1   b = 1   c = 3   d = 5

The worst thing you can ask an unresponsive person is "Why are you so quiet?" or "What do I have to do to get you to respond?" (a and b). You can leave the person alone temporarily and see what happens (c). But the best answer is to start asking about nonthreatening subjects (d) to draw the person out.

Your Score

1. _____   9. _____

2. _____   10. _____

3. _____   11. _____

4. _____   12. _____

5. _____   13. _____

6. _____   14. _____

7. _____   15. _____

8. _____

_____
Total Points

50–75 Points

You are self-confident and feel comfortable asking questions. You seek information and take action, no matter how difficult it may be. You are assertive, yet still able to establish long-term, supportive relationships with colleagues and clients, and you don't hesitate to ask others for help and advice.

40–50 Points

You are comfortable asking questions, but you don't seek the help and advice of others as often as you could. You feel that the best way to get more power is through your own achievement and recognition. To guarantee ultimate success, you need to listen more and to tune into new communication styles.

25–40 Points

You believe asking for help is a sign of weakness. When something goes wrong, you tend to blame circumstances or other people. Asking questions will reduce some of your anxiety, help avoid costly mistakes, and let you develop a more people-oriented approach to your career.

Less Than 25 Points

You tend to accept the blame for foul-ups, and you give up too easily. You are probably overworked and under stress. You avoid confrontation at all costs. Asking questions in nonthreatening situations will bolster confidence and give you a way to assert yourself without anxiety.

18 DOES YOUR TRAINING TRANSFER?

Scott Parry

Scott B. Parry, *Ph.D., is chairman of Training House, Inc. (Box 3090, Princeton, NJ 08540, 609-452-1505), a consulting and publishing firm specializing in human resource development with over 600 hours of packaged training programs. Scott is author of* **From Managing to Empowering** *(Quality Resources, 1994). He has conducted training programs in 24 countries on six continents.*

OVERVIEW

Instruction is effective only to the degree that new learning is converted into performance back at work. This process is known as **transfer.** Many factors influence the degree of transfer and determine the return on your training investment. The *Transfer Evaluation Instrument* contains a description of 50 factors that influence the transfer of training. They are grouped under five major headings:

✓ Course Design

✓ Instructor's Skills and Values

✓ Trainees' Abilities and Perceptions

✓ Workplace Environment

✓ Management and Supervisory Roles

Use the following assessment to evaluate a specific course and the degree to which training transfer is likely to take place. The *Transfer Evaluation Instrument* can be helpful whether you are planning a new course or evaluating an existing one.

TRANSFER EVALUATION INSTRUMENT

Directions: Circle the rating that best describes the training course that you are evaluating using the following scale:

2 = strong; no problem with this factor

1 = moderate; this factor is present, but needs improvement

0 = weak or absent; this factor is negligible or nonexistent

For example,

To what degree does the trainee's supervisor know what was taught and look for ways to reinforce new behavior on the job?   2   1   0

In this example, suppose that the supervisors of your trainees have themselves been through the course or a briefing before you launched the course for their people. They are very supportive and encourage their people to apply the things that they learned in class. Thus, you would circle 2.

Now suppose that the supervisors believe in training but are not very well acquainted with the course and what their people are learning to do. They give general encouragement, but cannot be as specific in their feedback and reinforcement as they should. You would circle 1.

Now suppose that the supervisors were too busy to concern themselves with the course and the things that their people learned from it. They spend little if any time recognizing and reinforcing new behavior when their people come back from a course. You would circle 0.

One hundred possible points can be obtained in scoring the instrument. How well will you rate?

1. How relevant is the content to the trainees' needs?   2   1   0
2. How appropriate are the instructional methods and media?
   2   1   0
3. Are there enough job aids, checklists, references, and the like, for use on the job?   2   1   0
4. How effective are the learning facilities and equipment?   2   1   0
5. How well do the trainees like the course design?   2   1   0
6. Is the length of the course appropriate to its objectives?   2   1   0
7. Do trainees have enough time in class to practice and refine new skills?   2   1   0
8. How smooth is the flow and transition from one session (topic, lesson) to the next?   2   1   0
9. Do trainees get enough feedback to help them to check progress and make corrections?   2   1   0
10. What kind of image does the course have throughout the organization?   2   1   0

Total of the 10 numbers circled above: _____

Instructor's Skills and Values

11. How well does the instructor know the subject and the work environment of the trainees?   2   1   0
12. To what degree does the instructor use language, examples, and analogies that the trainees can relate to?   2   1   0
13. Does the instructor spend additional time when trainees are having trouble learning?   2   1   0
14. To what degree did the instructor teach deductively (Socratic method and not inductive lecture method)?   2   1   0
15. How effective is the instructor's skill in keeping the class interactive and well paced?   2   1   0
16. Does the instructor have the respect of management and the trainees' supervisors?   2   1   0
17. To what degree does the instructor have the learners doing things rather than talking about how to do them?   2   1   0
18. How well do the trainees like the instructor as a person?   2   1   0
19. Does the instructor follow up after the course to see where trainees can or cannot apply what they learned?   2   1   0
20. To what degree does the instructor prepare trainees to deal with barriers (problems, frustrations) that they face back at work?
    2   1   0

Total of the 10 numbers circled above: _____

21. How favorable is the trainee's attitude toward the course and the work it prepares him or her for?   2 1 0

22. To what degree do the trainees possess the necessary prerequisites (entering behavior)?   2 1 0

23. Are members of the trainee's work group practicing the skills and concepts being taught?   2 1 0

24. How free are trainees of personal handicaps or problems that disrupt their concentration on the course?   2 1 0

25. To what degree do trainees see themselves rather than the instructor as responsible for their learning?   2 1 0

26. How stable is the trainee's job status and personal status (marital, health, and so on)?   2 1 0

27. How clear is trainee on how the course will be teaching new ways of doing things?   2 1 0

28. How committed are trainees to learning and applying new ways of doing things?   2 1 0

29. Do trainees have the abilities (courage, insight, verbal skills, and the like) to stop the instructor when they don't understand?
    2   1   0

30. How does the trainee perceive the rewards (benefits and such) of applying the new learning back on the job?   2 1 0

Total of the 10 numbers circled above: _____

31. How well do the workplace norms (expectations, culture, climate) support the new behavior?   2   1   0

32. To what degree did the timing of the training agree with the opportunity to apply it at work?   2   1   0

33. Do the physical conditions in the workplace support the desired behavior?   2   1   0

34. How readily does the course content translate into appropriate behavior on the job?   2   1   0

35. How permanent and resistant to change are the policies, procedures, equipment, and the like?   2   1   0

36. To what degree do peers and other employees support the trainee's new behavior at work?   2   1   0

37. How frequently do the trainees get to apply on the job what they learned during training?   2   1   0

38. To what degree do trainees receive frequent and specific feedback in the weeks following training?   2   1   0

39. How well understood are the rewards and penalties associated with performance?   2   1   0

40. To what degree does the course have the respect of the trainees' peers and supervisors?   2   1   0

Total of the 10 numbers circled above: _____

41. How strongly do managers and supervisors believe in the course and those who give it?   2 1 0

42. To what degree do supervisors want their trainees doing things the way they learned in class?   2 1 0

43. Do supervisors explain the value of the course before their trainees attend?   2 1 0

44. To what degree are supervisors rewarded by their managers for coaching?   2 1 0

45. Are assignments made so as to give trainees immediate opportunities to apply their new learning?   2 1 0

46. To what degree do supervisors send trainees to the right courses at the best timing, based on need?   2 1 0

47. Are supervisors taking time to recognize and reinforce the trainees' new behaviors back on the job?   2 1 0

48. To what degree do supervisors provide good role models by practicing what is taught in the course?   2 1 0

49. How well do supervisors understand the objectives and content of the course?   2 1 0

50. To what degree do supervisors have a development plan for each subordinate that includes training?   2 1 0

Total of the 10 numbers circled above: _____

Total of the five subtotals (out of a possible 100): _____

DO YOU NEED AN ELECTRONIC PERFORMANCE SUPPORT SYSTEM?

Barry Raybould

Barry Raybould *is president of Ariel PSS Corporation (100 View Street, Suite 114, Mountain View, CA 94041, 415-694-7880), an international consulting firm specializing in performance support, system design, and development methodologies. Barry is one of the early pioneers in the field of electronic performance support systems (EPSS) and has designed award-winning systems for many Fortune 500 corporations. He is a frequent presenter at national conferences and author of numerous articles and papers on the subject of EPSS. He is currently working on a new book on EPSS, as well as an interactive CD-ROM version.*

OVERVIEW

An electronic performance support system (EPSS) is the electronic infrastructure that captures, stores, and distributes individual and corporate knowledge assets throughout an organization, to enable an individual to achieve a required level of performance in the fastest possible time and with minimal support from other people.

Do you need performance support to stay competitive? Is your organization ready for electronic support? The following assessment checklist will help you to identify the questions that you need to ask to determine when an EPSS may be an appropriate solution to meet your organization's needs.

THE EPSS CHECKLIST*

Ask yourself whether the following items apply to your organizational situation. If you check at least 10 items, performance support may be worth considering. If you check 20 items or more, your organization should definitely consider following an electronic performance support strategy to meet its training, development, and informational needs.

External Business Environment

_____ Competition is increasing the need for improved customer service.

_____ Government or industry enforces quality or other standards.

_____ An increasingly complex marketplace requires your organization to expand its knowledge.

_____ Competitors offer better products or services.

_____ A dynamic business climate requires your organization to be very responsive to change.

Internal Business Environment

_____ The organization is downsizing.

_____ The organization mandates total quality management (TQM).

_____ The organization is acquiring or introducing new business units.

_____ The organization frequently introduces new products or services.

_____ The organization is reengineering key business processes.

_____ The organization has set high productivity improvement targets.

_____ The organization is combining functions in order to streamline client contacts or business processes.

*Adapted from Performance Support Engineering International Inc., *When to Use Electronic Performance Support—A Checklist*, The PSE Library™, edited by Barry Raybould, Publication no. TO68. Performance Support Engineering International Inc, 1995. Distributed on the World Wide Web http://www.epss.com or (500) 677-3438.

The Work

_____ Employees use computers in their work.

_____ A large percentage of the job is "knowledge work."

_____ Far more knowledge is required to perform the work than can be absorbed during training.

_____ Factors contributing to high job performance are known and understood.

_____ Job competence does not depend on sensory communication, such as touch or body language.

_____ Commonsense reasoning is not the job's most important component.

Job Performers

_____ The organization experiences high employee turnover and frequently changes job definitions.

_____ There is a large gap between the best and worst job performers.

_____ The best job performers are motivated and articulate enough to add knowledge to the system.

_____ Both workers and management think job performance is inadequate.

Information Access

_____ Workers use complex and changing information to do their jobs.

_____ Workers don't have quick access to information, because it is stored in many different forms—such as electronic databases, printed procedures, and people's memories—and in many different places.

_____ Key business information is not in electronic form.

_____ Most managers and job performers know what to do once they have the right information in hand.

Organizational Structure

_____ Workers in the organization are geographically dispersed.

_____ The organization is becoming flatter.

_____ Expertise is focused in small, geographically separated groups.

_____ Employees at different locations have different degrees of access to knowledge.

Information Systems

_____ The organization is introducing new hardware and software systems.

_____ The organization is moving from mainframe to client–server applications.

_____ The information systems department tries to make its systems easier to use.

Training and Human Resource Development

_____ Generalized training courses do not meet specific needs of different audiences.

_____ Training budgets are being cut.

_____ More or longer training programs do not improve performance enough.

_____ The organization is focusing on on-the-job training.

Documentation

_____ Documents are not specific enough to meet the needs of different audiences.

_____ The costs of producing and distributing paper-based documentation are high.

_____ Increasing the number and quality of documentation does not improve performance enough.

_____ The organization is focusing more on on-line documentation.

WHO IS COMPUTER LITERATE IN YOUR WORKPLACE?

20

Michaeline Skiba

Michaeline Skiba *is a training and development manager with experience in both the service and manufacturing industries. Her area of expertise is instructional design, with particular emphasis on formative education and survey instrument development, and electronic media production management. Mickey is currently a doctoral candidate in the Communication, Computing and Technology Department of Teachers College— Columbia University. She can be reached at 164 Dove Lane, Middletown, CT 06457, 203-632-1562.*

OVERVIEW

What software products do the people in your organization use most frequently on the job? How did they learn to use such products? Are they using them effectively? And is the systems staff providing the kind of help and support that your organization needs most? These are but some of the questions asked in the following assessment instrument. Use the *Computer Resources Survey* to gain valuable information about how computer services and computer products are actually being put to use within your organization.

COMPUTER RESOURCES SURVEY

The following questions are designed to gain a better understanding of how you use our organization's computer resources. The survey covers information about both computer products and services. But, first,

1. What is your job title? _____

2. In which department do you work? _____

Computer Products

3. On a scale from 1 to 7, indicate *how often* you use the following software products. On this scale, 1 = never and 7 = very often. You may, of course, choose any number in between that comes closest to your opinions.

	Never						Very Often
a. Windows	1	2	3	4	5	6	7
b. MS Word 2.0	1	2	3	4	5	6	7
c. MS Word 6.0	1	2	3	4	5	6	7
d. Quatro Pro for Windows	1	2	3	4	5	6	7
e. Power Point 4.0	1	2	3	4	5	6	7
f. Harvard Graphics	1	2	3	4	5	6	7
g. DOS 6.0	1	2	3	4	5	6	7
h. Lotus for Windows	1	2	3	4	5	6	7
i. Other [please specify the product(s)]:							
_____	1	2	3	4	5	6	7
_____	1	2	3	4	5	6	7
_____	1	2	3	4	5	6	7

4. To accomplish each of the following tasks, indicate which software product you *primarily* use:

   a. Create spreadsheets _____

   b. Design overheads for presentations _____

   c. Word process documents
   (e.g., letters, memos, manuals) _____

   d. Create graphs _____

   e. Design graphics (artwork) _____

   f. Set up a database _____

5. Software products are designed to accomplish a variety of tasks.

   a. When you are asked to complete a particular computing task, who usually determines the *method* by which you complete it? (Circle one.)

   Yourself   1   Your supervisor   2   A colleague   3
   Other   4 (please specify): _____

   b. Do you ever suggest an alternative approach? (Circle one.)

   Yes   1 (Answer c)   No   2 (Answer d)

   c. *Why* do you do so?

   d. What was the *main reason*?

6. How do you usually learn to use *any* type of software product? For each item, answer either "often," "sometimes," or "never."

	Often	Sometimes	Never
a. Take a course outside the company	1	2	3
b. Take a course while on the job	1	2	3
c. On the job, through trial and error	1	2	3
d. Self-taught by reading the user's instruction manual	1	2	3
e. Self-taught by using the product's built-in help features	1	2	3
f. Ask others for one-on-one help	1	2	3
g. Watch instructional videotapes	1	2	3
h. Other (please specify): _____	1	2	3

7. Using the items from the last question, please rank in order of preference the top three *methods* that you consider important to your personal learning style. (1 = the learning method you consider *most* important to your personal learning style; 2 = the *second most* important; and 3 = the *third most* important.)

   Rank

   a. _____ take a course outside of the company
   b. _____ take a course while on the job
   c. _____ on-the job, through trial and error
   d. _____ self-taught by reading the user's instruction manual
   e. _____ self-taught by using the product's built-in help features
   f. _____ ask others for one-on-one help
   g. _____ watch instructional videotapes
   h. _____ other (please specify):

8. Can you think of any software products or product features that should be added to those that exist at the present time?

   Yes   1 (Answer a)   No   2 (Answer b)

   a. What are the features   b. What are the *main reasons*
      you are looking for?   you desire these features?

   _____   _____

   _____   _____

   _____   _____

9. Using a scale from 1 to 7, indicate how you would rate the following types of computer *support services* provided by the information systems department. On this scale, 1 = never and 7 = very often. You may choose any number in between that comes closest to your opinions.

	Never						Very Often
a. You receive help when you need it.	1	2	3	4	5	6	7
b. Before a new product is installed on your computer, its capabilities are explained to you in a clear manner.	1	2	3	4	5	6	7
c. Systems employees respond to your *service* needs.	1	2	3	4	5	6	7
d. Systems employees are sensitive to your *business* needs.	1	2	3	4	5	6	7

10. How would you rate the systems *staff* on each of the following traits in terms of your own personal satisfaction?

	Excellent	Good	Fair	Poor	Don't Know
a. Positive attitude	1	2	3	4	5
b. Helpfulness toward customers	1	2	3	4	5
c. Timeliness and responsiveness	1	2	3	4	5
d. Accuracy of response	1	2	3	4	5
e. Overall customer service	1	2	3	4	5

11. In your own opinion:

a. What should *stay the same* as it is in the systems department?

b. What should be *changed* in the systems department?

12. How would you rate *yourself* on each of the following in terms of how you *usually feel*? Again, use a scale from 1 to 7, with 1 = never and 7 = very often. You may choose any number in between that comes closest to your opinions.

	Never						Very Often
a. I enjoy my job.	1	2	3	4	5	6	7
b. I enjoy the work that I do in my job.	1	2	3	4	5	6	7
c. I enjoy using a computer to do my work.	1	2	3	4	5	6	7
d. Usually, I complete my work within a normal 8-hour workday.	1	2	3	4	5	6	7

13. How long have you worked for the company? _____

14. How long have you used a computer to do your work? _____

Thank you for taking the time to complete this survey.

HELPFUL HANDOUTS

In this section of *The 1996 McGraw-Hill Training and Performance Sourcebook,* you will find nine "helpful" handouts. These handouts cover topics such as:

✓ Communication.

✓ Writing.

✓ Sales.

✓ Employee development.

✓ Training methods.

These handouts can be used as:

✓ Participant materials in training programs.

✓ Discussion documents during meetings.

✓ Coaching tools or job aids.

✓ Information to be read by you or shared with a colleague.

All the handouts are designed as succinct descriptions of an important issue or skill in performance management and development. They are formatted for quick, easily understood reading. (You may want to keep these handouts handy as memory joggers or checklists by posting them in your work area.) Most important of all, they contain nuggets of practical advice!

Preceding each handout is a brief overview of its contents and uses. The handouts themselves are on separate pages to make reproduction convenient.

It is helpful to read these handouts *actively.* Highlight points that are important to you or push you to do further thinking. Identify content that needs further clarification. Challenge yourself to come up with examples that illustrate the key points. Urge others to be active consumers of these handouts as well.

EMPOWERING EMPLOYEES FOR OPTIMAL PERFORMANCE

Ed Betof

Ed Betof, *Ed.D., is senior vice-president of MCAssociates (Mellon Bank Center, 1735 Market Street, 43rd Floor, Philadelphia, PA 19103, 215-563-7800), a consulting firm specializing in organizational change and leadership development. Ed is an adjunct faculty member of the Center for Creative Leadership and the Human Resource Planning Society. He is the lead author of* **Just Promoted! Surviving and Thriving in Your First Twelve Months as a Manager** *(McGraw-Hill, 1992).*

OVERVIEW

It is a commonly accepted notion today that optimal performance comes from empowered employees. What specifically do managers do to empower the people who report to them? This helpful handout makes six solid recommendations.

The suggestion list is useful for anyone who is in a supervisory, management, or team leader position. After reviewing the list, challenge yourself or those you train to think of at least three people whom they manage and determine how they would apply the six principles described to their own situations.

EMPOWERING EMPLOYEES FOR OPTIMAL PERFORMANCE*

Think or yourself as a catalyst striving for the best chemistry among you, your employees, and your work environment. Just as a farmer tends the soil, the empowering boss nurtures his or her people. Six critical elements will help you to build a positive self-fulfilling prophecy that results in high performance:

1. Challenge and "stretch" people.
2. Give people choices in how to get the job done.
3. Show respect for others.
4. Relate to people in a mutually supportive way.
5. Practice self-monitoring.
6. Build on successful experiences.

Challenge

From studies examining high-performance employees, we know that people tend to perform best when they need to "stretch" in their jobs. This usually means that people should be pushed (or preferably should push themselves) to work just beyond their own view of what is comfortable. "Just out of reach, but not out of sight" is an excellent rule of thumb. Managers and employees should agree to performance and achievement standards that provide stretch and that enhance high-level performance. The self-fulfilling prophecy comes into play here. People with low expectations usually work at that level. High expectations tend to result in high performance. Help your people to set goals that will help them to stretch.

*This handout was adapted from Edward Betof and Frederic Harwood, *Just Promoted! Surviving and Thriving in Your First Twelve Months as a Manager,* New York: McGraw-Hill, 1992.

We tend to perform best when we are allowed to develop our own best way to meet established standards and expectations. We are energized when we bring our own knowledge, creativity, and resources to the solution of a problem. This principle is true regardless of profession, industry, or type of organization. When General Schwartzkopf of Operation Desert Storm decided on a flanking movement to defeat Saadam Hussein, he required each division commander to develop the specific strategy for his division within the context of the larger plan. Dedicated employees in religious, human services, and educational institutions need to be able to tailor the way they work in order to support the missions and principles of their organization. Auto workers must feel that they have some control over the work flow, efficiency, and quality. Responsibility without control engenders resentment and defeat.

Respect

People with healthy self-concepts generally feel that they are respected by their peers and managers alike. Agreement or disagreement—even conflict, especially with new bosses, subsides when people feel that their opinions and ideas are respected. Organizations need a continual exchange of ideas. Better ideas are often forged from the white heat of disagreement. When we feel a foundation of mutual respect and support, we perform more confidently and use all our resources.

Mutually Supportive Relations

Empathy, the ability to relate to another's feelings and perceptions, is essential to empowerment. For years, psychologists have shown that the ability to put ourselves in the shoes of the other and understand another person's frame of reference is a critical factor in helping that person to achieve his or her potential. Managers need to understand and respect the perspectives of their employees, and employees need to understand and respect the perspective of the manager. Mutual respect is based on mutual understanding of needs and demands.

Employees need feedback on how well they are doing, and supervisors need information on what employees are doing. Monitoring and feedback are essential in helping employees keep track of how well they are meeting the challenge. Employee choice in getting the work done requires self-monitoring and personal responsibility for quality and output. Periodic checks on progress, process and quality, as well as coaching with reassessment and adjustment of work goals, help employees achieve their quality and quantity goals. Many managers also encourage peer monitoring, usually in team meetings where members discuss goals and achievements and their contribution to the team's accomplishments. This approach is also popular in self-directed teams.

Success Experiences

Success begets success! People who use their abilities in challenging situations are more consistently successful. They learn to use their capabilities, develop new skills and abilities, and determine what is required for success. Empowering leaders offer challenges that build on their people's successes and increase the chances for top performance under trying circumstances. Empowering leaders help their people to be successful. They set up an environment that encourages a positive self-concept and a feeling that we are fulfilling constructive and valuable goals.

These six elements, once established, can help leaders ensure high employee performance. Managers have an excellent opportunity to affect people in ways that can truly make a difference on the job. The process of "buying in" versus "dropping out" begins in the first days following your appointment as a manager. Employees work best when they are treated as if they are *able, responsible,* and *valuable.* Individuals often make the decision to be part of the solution rather than part of the problem within weeks, and certainly within a few months, of starting a new job or the arrival of a new boss. Employees who feel empowered become positive and creatively committed to their organization's success.

SEVEN WAYS TO REDUCE YOUR ACTIVE-LEARNING PHOBIA

22

Sivasailam Thiagarajan

As president of Workshops by Thiagi (4423 East Trailridge, Bloomington, IN 47408, 812-332-1478), **Sivasailam (Thiagi) Thiagarajan,** *Ph.D., specializes in designing and delivering training for improving human performance. Thiagi has been the president of the National Society for Performance and Instruction (NSPI) and of the North American Simulation and Gaming Association (NASAGA). He is the author of 24 books, over 175 articles, and several hundred games and simulations.*

OVERVIEW

Almost every trainer intellectually accepts the effectiveness of active learning. The idea that we learn best by *doing* is well recognized. When participants figure out things by ourselves, actually practice skills, and perform tasks that depend on the knowledge that they have, learning is deeper and longer lasting. However, many trainers are still unsure about using active-learning activities in their training sessions. It can be uncomfortable and even downright terrifying to switch from lecturing to role playing, gaming, action learning assignments, skills practice, and so forth, both for the trainer and the participants. If you have active-learning phobia, the following handout offers seven helpful suggestions. The tone is light, but the advice is therapeutic.

SEVEN WAYS TO REDUCE YOUR
ACTIVE-LEARNING PHOBIA

1. *Rational therapy:* Sit down in a quiet corner with paper and pencil (or a tape recorder). List the reasons why you are afraid of using learning activities. Here are some typical reasons:

   ✓ Making a fool of yourself

   ✓ Losing control of the participants

   ✓ Encouraging bizarre behaviors

   ✓ Forgetting an important step in the activity

   ✓ Being labeled as a touchy-feely type

   ✓ Being attacked by colleagues

   Dispute these spurious reasons by telling yourself things like this: "I may want not to make a fool of myself, but it is silly for me to feel desperate about it. So what if I make a fool of myself? The sky is not going to fall down!"

2. *Worst-case scenario:* Instead of disputing your fears, surrender completely and wallow in self-pity. Exaggerate your fears. For example, imagine that all your participants are from hell. Visualize their obnoxious behavior. Mentally picture total chaos in your classroom. Keep exaggerating your fears until you realize how silly you are—and burst out laughing.

3. *Systematic desensitization:* Visualize a positive session in which you are effectively conducting a learning activity with an enthusiastic group. Now create five or six scenarios that gradually become less positive and more negative. Your last scenario should be the worst possible fiasco. Return to your most positive scenario. If you feel any tension, relax by paying attention to your breathing or by tensing and relaxing your muscles. When you feel completely relaxed while holding the image, move on to the next scenario. Practice relaxing while visualizing increasingly frightening situations. Don't push yourself. You may need a number of days (or weeks or months) until you have desensitized yourself completely.

4. *Face the truth:* Whenever conducting a learning activity, remind yourself of these facts:

   ✓ Learning activities shift the participants' focus away from you and toward the activity.

   ✓ During a learning activity, you have plenty of free time to get ready for the next step.

   ✓ Peer pressure among the participants will keep the obnoxious people under control. You don't have to worry about disruptive participants because the others will handle them.

   ✓ You don't have to follow all the steps of the activity. You have complete control and you can change anything you want to.

5. *Affirmative pinch:* Think of the last time you had a positive experience in front of a group. Visualize this experience vividly. Hear the sounds, smell the smells, feel the feelings, and taste the taste of this memory clearly. See the faces of the participants. Listen to what they are saying. Listen to the background noises. Recapture your feeling of controlled flexibility. When your feelings are at a positive peak, press your thumb nail on the top joint of your little finger until it hurts slightly. Whenever you feel anxious while conducting an activity, repeat the thumb nail press to trigger a recall of your affirmative memory.

6. *Be playful:* It is ironic for you to take a learning activity too seriously. By definition, most learning activities (such as games, simulations, and role plays) require a playful approach. Focus on having fun and forget about the training objectives—temporarily.

7. *Understand the situation:* You need to understand these three things before you can effectively conduct a learning activity: the details of the subject matter, the characteristics of the participants, and the steps of the process. Instead of worrying about what is going to happen, spend your time learning more about these three things.

FIVE ACTIVE-LISTENING STRATEGIES

Cynthia Denton-Ade

As head of CDA Performance Systems (9850 Natick Road, Burke, VA 22015, 703-503-6679, CompuServe 74534,1077), **Cynthia Denton-Ade** *has 18 years experience designing and developing technical and management training. She works with industry and government clients to design training that maximizes student participation and learning. Cynthia conducts many workshops each year in instructor training, communications, and problem solving. She has held several offices in the National Society for Performance and Instruction (NSPI) and has won awards for her service.*

OVERVIEW

Success in most areas of the workplace greatly depends on one's ability to listen to others. Researchers claim that most oral communication is misinterpreted, misunderstood, or ignored. If fact, the average person listens with only 25% efficiency. Part of the problem is the gap between the rate at which people can speak (about 125 words per minute) versus the rate at which people can process information (about 300 words per minute). Anyone can learn to put this time to good use by using active-listening techniques.

This handout is a useful guide for anyone who must listen effectively to perform effectively. It contains five guidelines that you will want to integrate into your listening behavior.

FIVE ACTIVE-LISTENING STRATEGIES

There is a big difference between hearing and listening. Hearing is the process of receiving and decoding auditory input. Listening, on the other hand, refers to the process of making sense out of that auditory message. The purpose of active listening is to better understand the facts, ideas, and feelings presented by the person talking. This allows you to gather more accurate information and respond appropriately to people's questions and concerns.

Use the following five strategies to become an effective active listener.

1. *Let the person talk.* Most listeners talk too much. A large part of active listening is the art of staying silent. Silence allows the speaker time to express his or her message. Silence is uncomfortable for many listeners, so they compensate by interrupting, asking questions, or advising the speaker. Some listeners may stare blankly and unresponsively. Avoid both behaviors. Use the following four guidelines to take advantage of the silence and actively listen to the speaker.

2. *Use appropriate nonverbal responses.* Communication is encouraged when you show the speaker that you are listening. Try moving toward the speaker and leaning forward. Maintain an open position. Tightly crossed arms or legs can express defensiveness or closedness. While you are listening, maintain eye contact, and use nonverbal gestures such as nodding your head or comments such as "uh-huh" or "mm-hmm."

3. *Focus on both verbal and nonverbal messages.* Often people are communicating more than their words reveal. Listeners frequently miss many emotional components of a speaker's message. Watch for the speaker's facial expressions, gestures, and posture. Listen for the tone of the person's voice and the emphasis that they put on particular words. Although you cannot be sure of the speaker's emotions, you can make a good guess. You can check your understanding by using reflective questions.

4. *Paraphrase.* Paraphrasing shows the speaker that you are listening and allows you to confirm the speaker's message. To paraphrase, select the most important idea from what the person has said and put it into your own words. Avoid repeating the speaker's words verbatim; a summary of what the person has expressed is more appropriate.

If you think you know what the speaker is saying, then you might say,

✓ *What I hear you saying is …*

✓ *You mean that …*

✓ *As you see it …*

If you are not understanding what the speaker is saying, then you might say,

✓ *Is it possible that …*

✓ *As I hear it, you …*

✓ *Let me see if I understand …*

✓ *I get the impression that …*

Sometimes, reflecting the speaker's emotions is appropriate. For example, a student has just complained about a training exercise. You might say, "I am picking up that you feel frustrated that the exercises do not relate to your job."

5. *Ask probing questions.* Probing questions help the speaker focus in depth on a specific issue. Here are examples of probing questions.

✓ *Can you tell me more?*

✓ *What do you mean by that?*

✓ *Then?*

✓ *Can you give me an example?*

✓ *When does that occur?*

Make sure that your probes are open-ended. Open-ended questions require more than a yes or no response.

✓ *How do you feel about this idea?*

Not *Do you like this idea?*

✓ *Tell me how you see this problem?*

Not *Do you think this is a training problem?*

✓ *What happened when you came into the office?*

Not *Did your supervisor stop when you came in?*

BE YOUR OWN EDITOR

Harriet Diamond

Harriet Diamond *is president of Diamond Associates, Multi-Faceted Training and Development (123 Quimby Street, Westfield, NJ 07090, 908-232-2075), a firm that designs and delivers customized training programs and consulting services spanning all areas of communication and management skills. Harriet is the author of six published writing skills books (Barron's Educational Series, Inc.) and numerous published articles on oral and written communication. Diamond Associates works with industries including banking, pharmaceutical, transportation, utility, retail, health care, and casino and hotel.*

OVERVIEW

This is a helpful handout for those who never anticipated writing as part of their job descriptions and now find themselves overwhelmed when asked to write reports, proposals, or even letters. Recognizing that writing is one process and editing is another will relieve some anxiety.

The 12-step guide to editing that follows includes the following:

✓ Process

✓ Organization

✓ Sentence structure

✓ Punctuation

✓ Grammar and usage

✓ Positive language

✓ Active voice

BE YOUR OWN EDITOR

Most people tackle business writing under pressure to produce a document quickly. That's life. Most business writing, however, passes the scrutiny of one or more "editors." You can save time in the editing process if you accept the role of first editor.

The following is a 12-step guide to editing. Of course, even before step 1, you will identify your audience (reader) and purpose (reason for writing).

Step 1: Do not edit as you write. Imagine yourself wearing a beret—or any hat of your choice. That's your *writer's hat.* Keep it on.

Step 2: Write as the thoughts flow. Depending on your style, you may start and just keep going. You may write following an outline you created or the standard format of a document. Do not stop to locate the perfect word or the correct figure or date or to check your spelling or grammar. You are *writing,* not editing. Whether writing by hand or on line, keep that pencil or cursor moving forward!

Step 3: Remove your writer's *hat and put on your* editor's *visor.*

Step 4: Slowly read what you wrote. Does it make sense? Does it say what you intended it to say? Does it address your audience and your purpose?

Step 5: Is it well organized? Can you easily outline your writing piece? Does each paragraph focus on one topic?

Step 6: Review sentence structure. Is it varied?

Examples:

✓ Begin with an independent clause.

   Plant closings occur when production drops continuously.

✓ Begin with a dependent clause.

   When production drops continuously, plant closings occur.

✓ Use compound sentences.

   We bought new furniture, and we painted the office.

✓ Use simple sentences.

   Our meetings always begin and end promptly.

Step 7: Check punctuation. Some common concerns:

✓ Use commas correctly.

subject   verb   subject

Angie manages the accounting department, and Mark

       verb

supervises the credit division. (separated by a comma)

    subject   verb   verb

Suzanne conducts training programs and writes course manuals. (no comma)

✓ *Always* place periods and commas inside quotation marks.

His friends affectionately called him "Pretz."

✓ Add punctuation variety with the semicolon.

The reengineering process has affected every department; no one is satisfied.

We are launching several new loan packages and insurance options; therefore, product training is our priority.

✓ Check a style manual for hyphenated words.

Please use work-related examples.

Step 8: Check grammar and usage. Some common concerns:

✓ Subject and verb agreement:

No: *An audit of the records show a serious shortfall.*

Yes: *An audit (of the records) shows a serious shortfall.*

✓ Parallel structure:

No: *The new brochure is eye catching, easy to read, and has good information.*

Yes: *The new brochure is eye catching, easy to read, and informative.*

Step 9: Eliminate unnecessary words and phrases.

No: *In order to complete the renovation of the manufacturing facility, there has to be a temporary shutdown.*

Yes: *~~In order to c~~Complete~~ing~~ the renovation of the manufacturing facility requires a ~~there has to be a~~ temporary shutdown.*

No: *At this point in time, we recommend the renewal of the proposed contract and trust that our judgment meets with your approval.*

Yes: *~~At this point in time, w~~We recommend the renewal renewal of the proposed contract.~~and trust that our judgment meets with your approval.~~*

139

Step 10: Use positive language.

      No: *Don't forget to include directions.*

      Yes: *Remember to include directions.*

Step 11: Eliminate unnecessary or incorrect whiches.

      No: *Management canceled the meeting which was to determine our department priorities.*

      Yes: *Management canceled the meeting that was to determine our department priorities.*

Step 12: Use the active, not the passive voice.

      No: *Building materials were ordered last week.*

      Yes: *The project manager ordered building materials last week.*

CONDUCTING INTERVIEWS FOR R.E.S.U.L.T.S.

Bonnie Ferguson

Bonnie Ferguson *(504 Stillhouse Lane, Marlton, NJ, 609-985-5603) has held several positions at CIGNA and is currently the director of training and development in the Group Insurance Program. Her work has included classroom instruction, program design, group facilitation, and organizational consulting. Bonnie holds numerous certifications and particularly enjoys coaching and developing managers individually or in groups. She has recently focused her consulting on organizational communications issues.*

OVERVIEW

Interviewing! After a matter of mere minutes spent with a candidate, you must decide whether to hire someone in whom you and the company will invest considerable time and money. Few choices a manager makes are as critical or costly as selection decisions.

You need information—as much as possible about each candidate. Because research has shown that past behavior is the best predictor of future behavior, you will be looking for behavioral evidence. You will need to search for indicators that the candidate has demonstrated the attributes and abilities you are seeking.

The R.E.S.U.L.T.S. process, used completely and consistently, will guide you through the effort to make the best possible candidate selection. It is organized into three categories: planning for the interview, conducting the interview itself, and selecting the appropriate person for the job. Use this process the next time that you need to interview for R.E.S.U.L.T.S.!

INTERVIEWING FOR R.E.S.U.L.T.S.

Use this seven-step approach, spelled out with the letters R.E.S.U.L.T.S., to guide you through the process of planning and conducting interviews and selecting a candidate.

Review All Information to Plan and Prepare for Interview

- ✓ Start with (or create) job descriptions
- ✓ Update job information. Consult with Human Resource managers and other managers as necessary.

Establish Success Factors

- ✓ Consider and list the skills, attributes, and abilities necessary to do the job well.
- ✓ Scale the factors by importance. Be judicious about your "must haves."

Stop and Consider "Stoppers"

- ✓ List potentially strong negatives, such as a lack of flexibility, a dislike of working alone or on a team, or political naiveté.
- ✓ Add to your list of success factors. The "stoppers" may overshadow significant and relevant experience.

Planning Hints:

- ✓ Create an interviewing note-taking sheet that lists: success factors, "stoppers," behavioral evidence, and rating or rank.
- ✓ Compose questions and prompters to elicit substantial data rather than just a few words. Examples: "Tell me about a time when ..." or "Describe how you handled ..." Remember that hypothetical questions yield only hypothetical answers.
- ✓ Review each resumé in advance to focus your questioning strategy.

Utilize Interviewing Aids

- ✓ Assemble the question list and note-taking sheet you developed. Have the resumé available for reference. Share the resumé with any others who might be interviewing the same candidate.
- ✓ Take notes. This ensures accurate retention, especially if you are conducting interviews with multiple candidates.

Listen Carefully

✓ Dig for behavioral evidence with follow-up probes. Examples: "What did you do in the situation? What did you say? How did you feel?"

✓ Depart from your questioning strategy only when you find fertile ground for deeper probing.

Talk No More Than Necessary

✓ Speak no more than 20% of the time as the interviewer.

✓ Use your nontalk time for listening and taking notes.

Conducting Hints:

✓ Warm up the candidate with a "safe" topic such as the weather.

✓ Watch your time so that you devote most of it to information gathering, yet allow time for the candidate's questions.

Select a Candidate

✓ Review your notes (and other managers' notes, if applicable).

✓ Complete all ratings and then rank the candidates based on the success factors and "stoppers." Using weighting or prioritizing can help distinguish between two very qualified candidates.

✓ Include, but do not be governed by, a "gut" instinct.

✓ Make an offer to your candidate of choice.

Selecting:

Congratulations! Using the R.E.S.U.L.T.S. interviewing process, you have made the best possible selection decision. Remember to use this process every time that you are asked to interview a potential employee to ensure fair and thorough candidate appraisal.

A VACCINE FOR ACCELERATING LEARNING

26

Kevin Eikenberry

Kevin Eikenberry *is president of Performance Partners (7035 Bluffridge Way, Indianapolis, IN 46278, 317-387-1424, 73313.33@compuserve.com), a management and training consulting firm specializing in training trainers, instructional design, team building, and organizational learning. He consults with a wide range of organizations with 50 employees to Fortune 100 companies. Kevin is a board member of the North American Simulation and Gaming Association (NASAGA).*

OVERVIEW

Accelerated learning. There are lots of tools and techniques. And lots of talk. This checklist is not meant to make you an expert, but it will give you a "shot-in-the-arm" toward making the training you design and deliver more effective. If you are worried about getting sick (and lots of our training is sick or will be), your doctor may give you a shot, a vaccine of some sort, to help prevent the worst. On the next page is a list of suggestions and questions that may act like a vaccine—to prod, provoke, and produce new ideas to dramatically improve your training design and delivery.

A VACCINE FOR ACCELERATING LEARNING

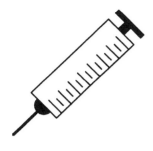

Think of **V**aried
       Active
       Collaborative
       Colorful and Creative
       Integrated
       Nontraditional
       Enjoyable   *to make your training more effective!*

Varied

To accelerate the learning in your sessions, recognize that different people have different learning styles, strengths, and preferences. Many models exist to elaborate on these differences, but the most important thing to remember is that, if people have different learning styles, a steady diet of the same teaching method(s) will not produce the best results.

Key Questions to Ask Yourself

✓ What are at least two new ways of helping people to learn the skills and knowledge?

✓ How can I reach visually oriented learners?

✓ How can I reach auditory learners?

✓ How can I reach kinesthetic (hands-on) learners?

✓ How can I balance theory with practical application?

Active

Learning is an active process. You cannot learn to ride a bicycle or to walk by only watching. And you cannot learn the skills in your lesson by passive means only.

Key Questions to Ask Yourself

✓ What different ways can I help people to practice skills?

✓ How can I stimulate curiosity and question asking?

✓ How can I make the sessions more mentally challenging?

✓ How can I use the knowledge of the group to teach themselves?

✓ How can I get the participants to be more physically active?

People may well learn more when studying and working together. They will also most likely enjoy the experience more. So let them do it! Find structured ways for the learners to collaborate.

Key Questions to Ask Yourself

✓ How can I get people to discuss the concepts among themselves?

✓ How can I create a safe environment for people to try and fail, give and receive feedback?

✓ What methods can I use to let participants work in different groupings?

✓ How can I build team support into the learning process?

✓ How can I help the group see me as a learning resource, rather than "the intruder"?

Colorful and Creative

OK, another "C" could have been childlike, but I cheated enough using both colorful and creative! Think back to grade school or kindergarten. Close your eyes and envision it. How was that classroom different from the one you train in now? Rich colors, lots of "stuff" to play with—a very stimulating environment, I would bet. How did it feel different? What was actually different? To accelerate learning, we need to keep people stimulated. Creative and colorful environments help do that.

Key Questions to Ask Yourself

✓ How can I stimulate and encourage creative thinking?

✓ How can I make the learning environment more colorful?

✓ How can I use music as a source of fun and enjoyment to support the learning?

✓ Are there thought-provoking or inspiring quotes or sayings related to the subject or skill that could be on the walls, on the tables, under the chairs, or in the learning materials?

✓ How can I make the learning environment a more pleasant, inviting place to be?

Integrated

No man (or woman) is an island. Neither should any of your subject matter be left unconnected from the learner's perspective. People need to see how the information and skills they are learning are linked together, and how they all relate to real life (be it their job, family, or whatever).

Key Questions to Ask Yourself

✓ How can I help people connect the new knowledge and skills to what they already know?

✓ How can I help people connect the learning to their work?

✓ How can I better connect the related content of the class?

✓ What analogies, metaphors, and stories can I use to improve retention and understanding?

✓ How can I help participants do application planning in class for improved results back in the real world?

Nontraditional

Attempting to accelerate the learning in your sessions will require you to do some things differently! This does not mean you are doing everything wrong now; it just means that to improve we must be willing to change. An environment where learning is accelerated will definitely be seen as nontraditional. In fact, people will probably see and feel it before the "class" even begins.

Key Questions to Ask Yourself

✓ How can I do the training in a totally fresh way?

✓ How can I get information across without lecturing?

✓ How can I help the learners to take more responsibility for their own learning?

✓ How can I change the physical arrangement of participants?

✓ How can I make the session less formal, and thus lower the student–teacher barrier?

Enjoyable!

People learn best when they are having fun. It's a simple fact. Yet far too often we won't allow work to be playful. We can accelerate learning when we help people to enjoy themselves.

Key Questions to Ask Yourself

✓ How can I build situations for natural laughter?

✓ How can I utilize games to make learning fun?

✓ How can I have more fun myself while helping others to learn?

✓ What can I do to make people *want* to be in this session?

✓ How can I create positive emotions and feelings for the learners about themselves, the new skills and knowledge, and the learning experience?

A CHECKLIST FOR SUCCESSFUL NEW EMPLOYEE ORIENTATION

Harriette Mishkin and Leah Sokoloff

Harriette R. Mishkin *is principal of Performance Concepts, 220 Locust Street, 21-B/C, Philadelphia, PA 19106-3946, 215-923-6925. Harriette designs and conducts management development workshops and consults with organizations on strategic planning and change initiatives. She was assisted by* **Leah J. Sokoloff,** *an associate in the firm who specializes in survey design.*

OVERVIEW

Giving importance to new employee orientation can immediately set the stage for superlative job performance and successful performance management. This helpful handout allows you to look at orientation as an ongoing process that involves the manager, the employee's co-workers, and the human resource staff in an effort to provide the best possible start for a new employee.

You will find that the process of new employee orientation is described from beginning to end. The suggestions begin with the actions that a person can take one week prior to the new employee's arrival and extend to the end of the first month on the job.

NEW EMPLOYEE ORIENTATION CHECKLIST

A new job is like a marriage, so make the most of the honeymoon period to encourage achievement early on. Use this suggested checklist to get ready for your new employee, plan first-day activities, and organize ongoing performance management strategies.

1. *One week prior to the new employee's arrival* is the time to prepare logistics, materials, and people. The purpose of these organizing activities is to ease the transition to the new job and new organization, for both the new employee and other department staff, and to provide a welcoming atmosphere. Being ready also signals that work and your role as supervisor are taken seriously.

_____ Clear your calendar and schedule time together (2 to 3 hours, including lunch).

_____ Review pertinent personnel procedures and key administrative policies from your organization's employee handbook.

_____ Review the job description and prepare the initial assignment, which should include reading material on the organization.

_____ Make arrangements for work space, equipment, and supplies (including an in-house telephone directory and employee handbook).

_____ Secure a password to gain access to the computer network.

_____ Create an office name plate (temporary or permanent).

_____ Let others on the floor (unit, department) know of the person's impending arrival and job duties.

_____ Ask for a volunteer to act as a buddy. Buddies can accompany the new employee to lunch on his or her second day, provide organizational perspectives on culture and norms, and provide a link to the informal social network.

2. *On the day the new employee arrives,* be ready to devote a block of time to him or her to provide essential information and directives. Since time spent with the human resource department varies from one organization to another (time spent on forms, medical exams, building tour, organization-wide orientation), begin your day by first determining the estimated time of arrival of your new employee in your office. This sets the pace for the rest of the day.

_____ Determine from the human resource department the approximate time that the employee will arrive in your office.

_____ Welcome the employee to the organization and give a floor tour, introducing him or her to others in the department and close by, especially those with whom the employee will work. Point out the bathroom, exits, water cooler, and coffee area, and show the employee his or her new work space. A name plate should be in place.

_____ After the employee settles into his or her office, use your office to provide information on the who, what, when, where, how, and why.

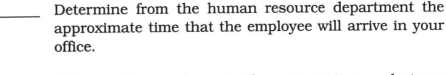

Who Who can answer my questions? Who will evaluate my work? Who are my co-workers? To whom do I go to when you are not here? To whom do I report? With whom will I work outside our department? With whom will I have lunch today? Who are all these other people and what do they do?

What Exactly what am I expected to do? What projects, products, and deadlines am I responsible for? What do they look like (if they've been done before)? What is the extent of my authority to make decisions? What key administrative, health, safety, security, and emergency policies immediately and directly affect me (smoking, eating, telephone, drug and alcohol, and the like)?

When When should I come in and leave? When are paydays, holidays, and the end of my probationary period? (Even though this information is given by the human resource department, familiarize yourself with the answers, since a lot of information is given the first day and not all of it is easily absorbed.)

Where Where is my work area? Where are the other units with whom I interact? Where are the rest rooms, lunchroom, and so on? Where is the copier, fax machine, supplies? Where do I hang my coat and secure my valuables (briefcase, handbag)? Where do I get coffee? Where is the water cooler?

How How do I answer and use the phone and take messages? How do I operate the photocopier and fax machine? How do I order supplies, fill out forms, or request something from other departments? How do I dress? How do I get paid? How do I send mail inside and outside the organization? How do I respond to requests from others?

Why Why do we follow that procedure (that is, time clock, security system, or other)?

_____ Take the employee to lunch (out of the building if possible) to continue a dialogue about the organization and to explain details she or he will not pick up from the reading material. Learn more about the person who now reports to you through careful and sensitive questions that do not overstep the bounds of the employer–employee relationship.

_____ Leave employee materials and work assignments to review, and check with him or her at least once before the end of day to answer questions and to give direction.

_____ Involve another department member in teaching the employee how to use equipment such as the fax machine, photocopier, computer network, telephone, and voice mail.

3. *By the end of the first week,* you and your new employee are ready to concentrate on the performance management relationship and your role as supervisor. You establish this relationship when you work together to determine the performance desired and agree on learning objectives. As a performance manager, you must create hands-on opportunities to teach tasks and delegate responsibilities. Starting this process early underscores its importance.

_____ Discuss the job coaching opportunities, performance counseling needs, and leadership (supervisory) style needed to enable the employee to perform effectively.

_____ Identify administrative policies and policies not already discussed (personal calls, travel policies, overtime, sexual harassment guidelines, grievance procedures, vacation, sick leave, and so on), and specific department procedures.

4. *During the second week,* you and your employee will begin to define expectations, standards, and outcomes. By then, you will have gained some perspective on what skills need to be developed, how much time it will take, and how much oversight you will need to provide.

_____ Set mutually agreed-to goals and objectives.

_____ Determine standards and expectations for quantity and quality, timeliness, and accuracy.

_____ Establish priorities and timetables.

_____ Determine a supervision schedule, for example, when time can be set aside to discuss projects and review progress.

_____ Discuss the evaluation process through timely feedback as well as through the yearly performance appraisal process.

5. *By the end of the first month,* you and your new employee have begun a professional relationship that requires you to begin coaching, monitoring progress, and tracking performance. Through the following activities, you will learn whether you need to reduce your efforts or can proceed to more complex and responsible assignments.

_____ Review assignments and be sure that they meet the stated goals, objectives, and standards.

_____ Update your situational leadership (supervisory) style depending on where the employee is in his or her task development.

_____ Confirm or change the supervision schedule based on employee task development needs.

_____ Maintain a documentation file of critical incidents for use in your ongoing role as coach and counselor and for performance appraisals. Indicate positive results as well as any concerns.

_____ Provide ongoing feedback in a timely and useful manner.

SEVEN KEYS TO SALES SUCCESS

Harriet Diamond

Harriet Diamond *is president of Diamond Associates, Multi-Faceted Training and Development (123 Quimby Street, Westfield, NJ 07090, 908-232-2075), a firm that designs and delivers customized training programs and consulting services spanning all areas of communication and management skills. Harriet is the author of six published writing skills books (Barron's Educational Series, Inc.) and numerous published articles on oral and written communication. Diamond Associates works with industries including banking, pharmaceutical, transportation, utility, retail, health care, and casino and hotel.*

OVERVIEW

This helpful handout discusses seven keys to successful selling that form a critical foundation on which to develop sales skills. While numerous books exist on all these keys, this aid gives an introduction to each.

The following keys to sales success are covered:

- ✓ Goals
- ✓ Belief
- ✓ Passion
- ✓ Communication
- ✓ Time management
- ✓ Lifelong learning
- ✓ Hard work

SEVEN KEYS TO SALES SUCCESS

Goals

If you don't know where you are going, how will you know when you get there? This question sets the stage for goal setting. Develop a plan. What do you want to accomplish? By when? How can you do it?

Your sales career can take you anywhere. Set long- and short-term goals to get where you want to go. Write your goals and put them where you can see them every day. This will serve as both a conscious and subconscious reminder. Soon your goals will take on a power of their own.

Belief

There is a direct relationship between how strongly you believe in a goal and how fast you accomplish it. Believe in yourself and in what you are doing. Act as if you will succeed and you *will* succeed. Reinforce your belief and project it by visualizing success before each sales encounter.

Passion

Passion is the greatest motivator of all—and it is contagious. Passion is also a catalyst for excellence. The more you love what you do, the greater your success will be. Success will boost your self-esteem, which, in turn, will continually lead you to success. It's an endless loop: passion → success → self-esteem → passion → success.

Communication

Master your communication with yourself and others.

Self-talk: We are constantly communicating with ourselves, and too often our self-talk is negative. For example, most people respond to mistakes with "How could I be so stupid?" or "That was so dumb!" Instead, we should understand that mistakes are a part of learning and examine what we learned from them.

Communication with others: Listen. By listening you can learn your customer's needs, your competitor's plans, and your market's direction.

Follow these steps to good listening:

Question

✓ Ask open questions to get complete information.

✓ Maintain eye contact.

✓ Give nonverbal cues: nodding, leaning toward the speaker.

✓ Respond when appropriate.

✓ Don't interrupt.

✓ Summarize.

Read Signals

Body language and verbal cues will tell you when your customer is ready—or not.

Respond to key signals.

Time Management

Your efficient use of time directly relates to your success. One of the simplest ways to use your time well is to consistently ask yourself, "Am I using my time wisely?" As a salesperson, your focus is on prospecting, presentation, and follow-up. If you organize your time so that you are always prospecting, presenting, or following up, you will always be on track.

Lifelong Learning

Salespeople tend to forget that they are professionals. Like doctors and lawyers, salespeople must keep up with their profession, industries, and products. Every day, read on a subject that will enhance your professional knowledge: sales, motivation, your industry, your product, your competition. In today's high-tech environment, you can also take advantage of audio and video tapes, as well as computer software.

Hard Work

Your plan is to build a successful sales career. While each of the preceding six keys is essential, we all know that nothing of great value can be built without hard work. Hard work alone, however, can get you on the fast track to nowhere; if you work hard *and* smart, there is no limit to where you can go.

TEN STEPS TO COMBAT PARTICIPANT RESISTANCE

Brooke Broadbent

Brooke Broadbent *is a training consultant specializing in instructional designs, technical writing, and project management. Brooke is the author of numerous courses, articles, books, and brochures about computer-related subjects, training methods, and occupational safety and health. He can be reached at 867 Explorer Lane, Orleans, Ontario, Canada, K1C 2S3 or broadb@magi.com or http://infoweb.magi.com/~broadb.*

OVERVIEW

Do your concerns about participants' skepticism give you precourse butterflies? Instructional designers, internal consultants, external consultants, trainers, and managers of trainers all encounter participant resistance at some point in their careers. Of course, not all learners resist new information, but those who do can complicate classroom dynamics.

You know from your predesign efforts that the new information in your training will help solve operational problems, but you might fear that participants will resist learning it. You know that some will feel like prisoners in your classroom, since they prefer the old way of doing things and they don't want training on new methods. Others don't care what you do because their skepticism turned to cynicism a long time ago. They are not going to change their ways.

The handout that follows identifies 10 steps for combating participant resistance. You can use the steps to design an entire training course or a single training module. Areas where the 10 steps can be used are unlimited, from sales and customer service training to organizational redesign and the introduction of new technology.

The 10 steps are not presented as a one-size-fits-all solution, but as guidelines to adapt to your situation. Follow these steps to design training that anticipates resistance, identifies participants' skepticism, and deals with potentially difficult situations head on.

TEN STEPS TO COMBAT PARTICIPANT RESISTANCE

Steps	Why?
1. Listen to potential participants. In the needs analysis phase, meet with potential participants in focus groups (±20) and/or individually (±10)	Potential participants have a lot to say to instructional designers if we take the time to listen. Individual meetings generate personal concerns, group meetings build synergy among ideas and help to paint a global picture of participants' concerns.
2. Identify the sources of skepticism. Be sure to gather information about skepticism when meeting with participants.	Problems never get solved if they are swept under the rug. It is important to identify what is behind participants' cold, empty stares.
3. Make copious notes about skepticism and any other significant information that you gather.	The only way to remember clearly what people say is to make notes as it is said.
4. Synthesize the negative comments. Place these comments on flip chart sheets.	Placing the comments on flip charts before the course saves time from doing this exercise during the course.
5. Use the flip chart sheets in the training. After the usual administrative and ice-breaking exercises, post the sheets, explaining that they reflect comments gathered during the individual interviews and focus groups.	By acknowledging the sources of skepticism, you have shown that you are concerned about the problems participants have faced. Using the posted sheets allows you to word skepticism carefully and to present it in a noninflammatory manner.
6. Give participants time to evaluate the posted statements. Individually, participants read the flip charts, deciding whether the statements of skepticism reflect their personal concerns.	By having participants read the statements of skepticism and identify their personal concerns, you help them to recognize their personal concerns.

Steps	Why?
7. Add participants' additional concerns to the list. Give participants an opportunity to add additional items reflecting their concerns.	This ensures that each participant sees the list as accurate.
8. Have participants select their main concerns from the posted list. They place colored dots beside the items corresponding to their personal concerns. (The instructor can use the colors of the dots to show order of significance. For instance, red for most important and blue for second most important.) (Or the instructor might decide to use red dots the first time doing the exercise, blue the second time, and so on, changing each time the course is delivered.)	Colored dots are fun to use and they provide a clear picture of participants' skepticism. The placing of these dots helps participants, instructors, and even policy developers clarify issues.
9. Leave sheets posted throughout the course, and use them to introduce segments of the course by pointing out how they address the concerns raised.	The flip chart sheets and participants' skepticism become a major focus for the course, adding purpose and symmetry.
10. At the end of the course, return to the posted sheets and summarize how the course has addressed participants' concerns.	This helps to answer participants' skepticism in an overall way. Participants leave the session convinced that their time has been well spent.

PRACTICAL GUIDES

In this section of *The 1996 McGraw-Hill Training and Performance Sourcebook*, you will find eleven practical guides. These "how-to" guides are short articles containing useful ideas and guidelines for implementing a team or organizational initiative.

You will find advice about such initiatives as:

✓ Coaching, supervising, and mentoring.

✓ Personal and career effectiveness.

✓ Training design and delivery.

✓ Management skills.

✓ Employee development.

Each guide contains step-by-step advice. Several have examples, illustrations, charts, and tables to enhance your understanding of the content. You will find that these guides are clearly organized and easy to read.

Four uses for the practical guides are suggested as:

1. Guidelines for your own consulting, facilitating, and training interventions.

2. Implementation advice to be shared with peers and people who report to you.

3. Recommendations to senior management.

4. Reading assignments in team building and organizational consultations and training programs.

HOW TO INCREASE COMPREHENSION AND RETENTION WITH 25 LEARNING STRATEGIES

Anne Marrelli

Anne Marrelli, *Ph.D., is a senior human resource consultant for General Motors Hughes Electronics (Loc. C0, Bldg C01, PO Box 80028, Los Angeles, CA 90080). Anne has published in* **Performance and Instruction** *and* **Technical and Skills Training** *and has received awards for instructional design from the National Society for Performance and Instruction (Los Angeles Chapter), the Government Finance Officers' Association of the United States and Canada, the Los Angeles County Productivity Commission, and the National Association of Countries.*

The following guide explains how you can increase trainees' comprehension and retention of new material by integrating specific learning strategies into classroom and computer-based or print-based courses.

Learning strategies are activities in which the learner manipulates new material to understand and remember it. This guide describes 25 learning strategies and elaborates on several of them through the use of specific examples.

Learning strategies activate the information processing functions of the brain. In order to learn, trainees must be personally engaged with the material. Learning is an individual, constructive activity. Passively listening to an instructor or reading text produces only superficial understanding and a low rate of retention.

You can use the 25 learning strategies that will be described in two ways:

1. *Incorporate the strategies into your training courses.*

   ✓ After you present each chunk or module of new material, use one or more of the strategies to help the trainees actively process the new material.

   ✓ Consider carefully what you want the trainees to learn when you select a learning strategy.

✓ Provide explicit directions for using each strategy. In a classroom, it is best to offer both oral instructions and instructions printed on a flip chart, overhead, or handout.

✓ Explain to trainees the rationale for each learning strategy.

✓ If possible, use the same strategies in several courses or course modules or suggest that trainees use the strategies in other courses. Practice in using the strategies increases their effectiveness.

✓ Have the trainees perform the strategies individually or in pairs. The strategies will only be effective if each individual actively participates. If you use small groups, some trainees may not be fully engaged in the activity.

✓ Allow for individual differences in preferred learning style. The three main learning styles are *visual* (learning by seeing), *auditory* (learning by hearing), and *kinesthetic* (learning through body movements). You might present two or more learning strategies for each chunk of new information and allow learners to choose the one that they think will be most effective.

2. *Teach the strategies in learn-how-to-learn courses or distribute copies of* 25 Learning Strategies *for trainees to try on their own.*

✓ Explain what learning strategies are and how they facilitate learning.

✓ Teach the trainees the learning strategies described here. Guide the trainees through demonstrations of each strategy.

✓ Include copies of these learning strategies in print-based or computer-based self-study courses or distribute them to trainees in classroom courses to use in individual study sessions.

25 LEARNING STRATEGIES

1. *Acronym:* Use the first letters of information to be memorized to form a word or phrase that can easily be remembered. *Example:* "Kings play chess on fine-grained sand" can help you remember the biological divisions of living things (kingdom, phylum, class, order, family, genus, species).

2. *Rhymes and songs:* Write short rhymes or tunes that contain the information to be learned. *Example:* "*I* before *e* except after *c*, except when you hear *a* as in neighbor and weigh."

3. *Flash cards:* Prepare your own flash cards on blank index cards and use the cards for practice. This technique is most effective if you speak aloud during practice. *Example:* To learn medical terminology, write a term on one side of a card and the definition on the reverse side.

4. *Draw pictures:* Draw a picture of the information to be learned. *Example:* To learn the names and locations of the glands in the human body, draw a picture showing each gland in its proper location and label it.

5. *Make a collage:* Make collages by gluing small objects or pictures cut from magazines, newspapers, and catalogs to depict information you are learning. *Example:* To learn the foods included in each food group of the nutrition pyramid, draw the pyramid, label each group tier, and paste in pictures cut from magazines of the foods included in each group.

6. *Move it:* Manipulate and arrange small objects to model a concept or a principle. *Example:* To learn the concept of a normal distribution in statistics, use dry beans to create a model of the normal curve. Glue the beans to a large sheet of paper and label the percentages under each part of the curve.

7. *Knowledge network:* Write key points on a sheet of blank paper, leaving white space around each point. Draw an oval around each point. Each oval is called a node. When you have listed all key points, select the node containing the point that you need to know first to understand the other points. Then pick a second node that is logically related to the first. Draw a line or arrow connecting the first and second nodes. Continue the network by connecting the nodes in the order that makes sense to you. Finish by connecting the first and last nodes.

8. *Mind maps:* As you read written material or notes taken in class, draw a map of the important concepts using key words, quick sketches, and symbols. Three possible formats: (a) Note each major concept as a spoke branching out from a wheel with subbranches for subordinate points. (b) Draw your map as a road with major concepts and accompanying sketches appearing in road signs. (c) Note the major concepts along a line that snakes back and forth from the top of the page to the bottom.

9. *Break it down:* Break difficult concepts or principles into smaller and smaller parts until the meaning is clear to you. Begin by writing the full concept or principle and enclosing it in an oval. Then, as you break the concept or principle down into smaller parts, write down each part and enclose it in a separate oval. Connect the ovals with arrows, beginning with the overall concept or principle and moving to the smallest part.

10. *Define it:* Prepare several copies of a definition worksheet with spaces to identify six types of relationships for concepts or principles: characteristics and descriptors, antecedents, consequences, evidence, subsets, and supersets. As you read or review new material, complete a worksheet for each key concept or principle.

11. *Double define it:* The "define it" strategy (item 10) can be used to compare and contrast concepts or principles by altering the worksheet to present two concepts or principles side by side. As you review the material, simultaneously identify the six relationships for both concepts or principles.

12. *Imaging:* Close your eyes and create a mental picture of the process or procedure that you are learning. The more detailed you make your image, the more effective the image will be in helping you to remember the correct procedure. *Example:* To remember a sequence of steps to follow in solving a customer service problem, visualize yourself going through each step. Picture the setting, the clothes you are wearing, the customer, the problem, and what you say and do in each step that you take in working with the customer.

13. *Radio commercial:* Write and present a radio commercial explaining to listeners the benefits and importance of a procedure or the key points of a concept or principle. *Example:* You are learning about the benefits of doing a job analysis of the duties and tasks of a position before designing an interview. Tell your listeners what a job analysis is and why it is important that they do one.

14. *Write a story:* Create a story using the important points you are learning. It can be a cautionary tale about the terrible things that happen to someone who does not follow prescribed procedures or a heroic tale about an employee who saves the day. Make it funny or serious. You can also tell your story to co-workers. *Example:* You are learning how to select the most qualified candidate for a job on the basis of past job behavior and other objective information, rather than your personal feelings or intuition. You write a funny story about an employer who ignores the principles you are learning, conducts a very poor interview, and ends up hiring a complete misfit.

15. *You are the expert:* Explain the important points of the new material that you are learning to a family member or friend in simple, everyday language. *Example:* You are learning the principles of total quality management. When you get home, explain the principles to your 10-year-old daughter in terms that she can understand.

16. *Memory flashing:* As you study new material, create a mind map (see strategy 8). When you have finished, put the map out of sight and re-create it from memory. Compare the new map with your initial map and revise the new map as needed. Twenty-four hours later, review the map for 5 minutes. Seven days later, review the map again for 5 minutes. Fourteen days later, review the map for 5 minutes. Then review the map monthly thereafter for 5 minutes.

17. *Personal plan:* Write a detailed and realistic plan for how you will apply the new material that you are learning to your job. State how you will apply the concepts, follow the procedures, or use new skills. If possible, also explain your plan orally to a colleague. *Example:* You are learning how to communicate more effectively with your employees. Plan what specific actions you will take to improve communication, such as scheduling weekly staff meetings, talking for a minute or two with every employee each day, practicing active-listening skills when meeting with employees, hosting monthly staff breakfasts, and so on.

18. *Organize it:* If you are learning new material that can be organized by categories, functions, activities, or other divisions, create charts, tables, or lists to help you to understand and remember the material. *Example:* You are learning the basics of managing a work group. You can list your responsibilities as a manager in a table divided into three columns labeled, "Leading," "Training," and "Providing Resources."

19. *What is it like?* Compare point by point the new material that you are learning to something familiar in your work or personal life. Write down the similarities or explain them to a co-worker. *Example:* You are learning how to work effectively in a team. You can compare the operating principles of commitment to team goals, continuous communication, pooling your resources, reaching consensus, and resolving conflicts with the similar principles required for a happy marriage.

20. *Give me an example:* Write down as many examples as you can of the new concept that you are learning, then list nonexamples. Instead of writing, you could work with a friend, taking turns calling out examples and then nonexamples. *Example:* If you are learning how to conduct a cost–benefit analysis and need to understand the concept of cost components, you could list several examples of costs incurred by your work group for a project. For nonexamples, you would list several items that are not costs but belong to another category, such as benefits or cost savings.

21. *Take notes:* Prepare several copies of a note-taking outline with spaces for you to list the key idea, important points, supporting evidence, examples, and how you could apply this information to your work. As you study new material, complete an outline sheet for each major chunk of information.

22. *Rehearse it:* After you review your course notes or read about a topic, put the material away and explain to yourself what you just read. Say it in your own words and add your own examples or how you would use the information on the job. Then go back and read the material again to check if you left out any important points.

23. *Cross-examine it:* After you read new material or review your notes from class, ask yourself the following questions or discuss them with a co-worker. Answer the questions out loud even if you are working by yourself.

   ✓ Do I agree with the author (or instructor)? Why?

   ✓ Have I seen an example?

   ✓ Have I seen a counterexample?

   ✓ What questions or criticisms do I have?

   ✓ How can I apply this information to my work?

24. *Ask questions:* After studying new material in class or in a text, take 10 or 15 minutes to review the material and write several questions about it. Work with a partner and take turns asking each other the questions you have prepared.

25. *Act it out:* Work with a partner to prepare a role play or skit demonstrating a behavior or procedure that you are learning. *Example:* If you are learning how to conduct good performance appraisal meetings with your employees, you can prepare a role play demonstrating how to conduct an effective meeting.

HOW TO ENGAGE IN COACHING AND MENTORING*

Linda Wingate and Ann Scanlan

Linda C. Wingate *is a founding principal of Dimensions in Leadership (413 South Carlisle Street, Philadelphia, PA 19146, 215-731-1405), a firm specializing in identifying, assessing, and developing future leaders. Her experience includes 17 years with Fortune 500 insurance and financial services firms. She is currently president of the Philadelphia Human Resource Planning Group (PHRPG).* **Ann E. Scanlan** *is a corporate human resource manager at U.S.F. & G. Company (100 Light Street, Baltimore, MD 21202, 410-234-2271). Her professional human resource experience has been in manufacturing, retailing, publishing, managed care, insurance, and financial services.*

Coaching and mentoring. Both words are heard frequently throughout the business environment, but what exactly do these words mean? Have you ever been appropriately "coached" on a job? How does being coached differ from being simply managed? And how does being a mentor vary from being a friend? These questions and more are answered in the following guide, which provides definitions of coaching and mentoring, how-to's and hints for both the employee and the manager, and quotations from individuals who have actually been in the position of coach or mentor. Read on to discover how you can change an ordinary employee–manager relationship into an experience that has the potential to reap positive rewards throughout an entire career.

A *coach.* The label is intended to bring into the business environment the image of an individual on the sidelines, continually encouraging and pushing you to do far more than you ever believed you could. The coach is actively involved in the ground level nature of your work, showing you on a real-time basis where adjustments are needed to per-

*The information in this guide was based on a research study conducted at CIGNA in which 70 senior managers and executives were interviewed on the subject of coaching and mentoring. CIGNA refers to CIGNA Corporation and/or any of its subsidiaries. Insurance and related products are provided only by its insurance company and other subsidiaries, which employ most CIGNA employees. Quotes from employees within this guide are used to illustrate behaviors and specific coaching and mentoring situations. The quotes were taken directly from interview transcripts.

fect your performance. Alternatively, a *mentor* has a longer-range view of both you and your career and works to encourage an individual to develop expertise, take risks, and look for career-enhancing opportunities. A coach is a supervisor or manager who helps you to see more than just the immediate tasks on hand; a mentor extends the relationship with employees who may or may not be direct reports. In both cases, the relationship depends on you and your coach or mentor to play an active role and receive the mutual benefits of broad support.

Finding a coach or mentor at work is just one aspect of your entire career development process. As you consider your job performance, keep in mind that the first step in your development is to do your current job well. The best indicator of how well you will do another job is how well you are doing currently. Sometimes the job you want may be the one you have; all that is needed is an enlargement and enrichment of your current responsibilities. Sometimes a lateral move is a useful way for you to broaden your skills and abilities and provide new challenges.

A second aspect of your career development process is to keep in mind that your most important ally at work is your boss. Managers can directly affect your daily life and career advancement. In addition, supervisors or managers can teach you valuable lessons about organizational values and politics. Whether you learn from their individual strengths or weaknesses, the unique lessons offered by a supervisor or manager can only come from exposure to a variety of bosses, as opposed to assignments themselves.

As you consider your overall career progress and goals, keep the following points in mind:

Tips for Individual Career Development

✓ Take into consideration your personal life values in career decision making.

✓ Consider taking assignments that no one else wants. They can provide valuable learning and at times high visibility.

✓ Develop a core functional expertise early on and do it better than anyone else.

✓ Get leadership experience early in your career.

✓ Nurture and maintain good peer relationship; be a team player.

✓ Maintain professional decorum and dress appropriate to your office culture.

✓ Seek out people who can answer questions for you or refer you to others who can.

✓ Ask for performance feedback if you don't know how you are doing.

✓ Be positive when you receive feedback—remember, it will help you to get where you want to be.

✓ Increase your network by volunteering for task forces or other special projects.

✓ Look for coaching or mentoring from your peers or previous supervisors when your current supervisor cannot meet your needs.

✓ Try to identify senior managers who would be good role models.

✓ Consider development-in-place by enriching or enlarging your current job.

You have developed a core expertise, taken positions of leadership, volunteered for special projects, and generally feel as though your career is on track. So why include the additional investment of time and energy into a coaching or mentoring relationship? Here are three first-person testimonials as to why such a relationship can be so valuable to your individual development:

"My coach spent time after business hours with me. He helped me rehearse a very important presentation that had some bad news. He also helped me frame the message so that my audience, who was older and more experienced than I, would accept it. I earned their respect and after that I had regular contact with senior management."

"I had a former manager who I consider a really good mentor. We both remained in the same company, but I no longer work for him. He would stop by my office from time to time for a visit. His greeting was always the same: 'I bring you truth.' During the course of our visit he would give me feedback about how I was perceived, how certain projects were running, and generally what the 'book' was on me. Upon leaving, his farewell was always the same: 'Remember, I only bring you truth.' What I gained and learned from these visits was invaluable. The timely feedback gave me an advantage: I modified behaviors, mended fences, and tried new ways of doing things. I still keep in touch with my mentor who is now a good friend."

"Early in my career I had a boss who gave me the opportunity to present to a very important account that I had been working on for many months. I can remember the feeling when the limo pulled up to take us to New York for the presentation. I was nervous but well prepared. I made sure to always give 150% to everything I did. I was very young and this was my first big 'in person' client experience. My boss assured me it would be my show and that he would be there to lend support. It was a very successful meeting. Years later when I successfully competed for a sales management job, this former coach and mentor came to me and said, 'I had no doubt that you would get the job. I knew you had the right stuff years ago when you made that presentation!' This has always stayed with me: 'the importance of doing the very best possible job no matter how junior you are.' Someone always notices."

How do you open yourself up to the possibility of being coached or mentored? Here is a list of key behaviors evidenced by employees who have made themselves receptive to a supportive relationship with a direct or indirect manager.

✓ Be willing to take risks and to take on work not done before. Define your own jobs and do not limit yourself to how others have done the job if you can do it better.

✓ Take advantage of opportunities and do not wait to be told what to do. Take responsibility for your own career and initiate the first step in getting what you want.

✓ Try to learn something from every job you have and every supervisor or manager with whom you work. Focus on learning as much as possible about the business and make the most out of having a "bad boss" or a "lousy assignment."

✓ Work hard to do your current job well, rather than focusing on next steps. Hard work earns you credibility and respect in the eyes of senior management.

✓ Expect success and work hard to get it. Demonstrate confidence, adaptability, and stamina in difficult situations.

You have found a manager who has worked hard to coach you to be your best. A mentoring relationship with a higher-level employee has enabled you to see the big picture and plan for the next steps in your career. So how do you return the favor to other individuals? How do you distinguish what you have been doing from what you could be doing to support the employees that work for you? Here is a list of roles that expand on the conventional authoritative, directive modes of responsibility in which managers often find themselves at work.

Helping Roles for Supervisors and Managers

Coach and mentor: The majority of mentors are good coaches. They provide guidance and advice and serve as special sounding boards. They take chances on people who demonstrate potential and ability. They create a safe environment where trust is established. They spend time with their protegés to help them learn.

Technical tutor: The tutor or teacher knows a great deal about the business and guides employees in the technical areas, such as financial, underwriting, and claims. These relationships are generally short-lived and sometimes develop into other business relationships or end when the individual becomes technically proficient.

Patron and sponsor: The patron is higher in the management chain and is an advocate for the individual. Often this person's identity is not known to the individual.

Friend: Friendships develop between individuals, whether they are the immediate boss or more senior manager, peers and associates, or people outside the organization, that is, customers. The majority of friendships are business-related.

As you can see from this list, a variety of roles is available to you in your job as a supervisor or manager that are extensions of what you might normally consider to be within the duties of your position. The worth of expanding your position beyond its regular confines can only be appreciated if you have had someone else coach, mentor, tutor, sponsor, or befriend you on the job. Think about how someone else has gone the extra mile for you, and it is easy to begin the process of helping another.

Here is a list of behaviors to help guide your coaching and mentoring activities with yourself in the management role.

Key Behaviors of Coaches and Mentors

✓ Give employees work in areas of interest to them.

✓ Ask questions to help employees think through complicated projects instead of just telling them what to do.

✓ Tell employees about your own experiences and the lessons learned to help them in similar situations.

✓ Work alongside employees on a project to teach them new skills or help them get the work done on time.

✓ Let employees know if there are ways that they can improve the quality of their work or improve the way that they interact with others.

✓ Talk with employees about their career interests and what they will need to do to get the jobs that they want.

✓ When possible, introduce employees to others who can help them to get the jobs that they want.

Going from the general to the specific, here is a list of ways that you can immediately begin instituting a coaching or mentoring strategy on an everyday basis for your employees.

On-the-Job Opportunities for Coaching and Mentoring

Project work: When assigning work, make sure that both veteran and junior employees get access to development tasks. Don't always assign the same tasks to the same people; balance routine tasks with new tasks to broaden each employee's repertoire of skills.

Meetings: Invite an employee who has been involved in a particular project to attend more senior level meetings at which the project will be discussed. Spend time with employees before important meetings to give them advance notice and advice about some of the questions or concerns that might be raised.

Presentations: Invite employees to make presentations about projects or topics that interest them or in which they played a key role. Use presentations to allow employees to shine. Stay in the background and let them take ownership and credit for their accomplishments and ideas.

Task forces: Allow employees who have mastered their current jobs to learn more about the organization and to get exposure to senior managers by appointing them to a task force or a highly visible project. Assist employees with their task force assignments by sharing your knowledge of different parts of the organization and introducing them to others who have the information that they need.

Finally, the following list of ideas will help you to improve on your coaching and mentoring abilities for the length of your career.

How to Improve Your Coaching and Mentoring Skills

✓ Take responsibility for providing feedback to an employee regarding skills, abilities, and developmental actions.

✓ Open doors and set up contacts for employees to establish career-advancing contacts.

✓ Create opportunities for employees to demonstrate their competence. Delegate assignments that stretch knowledge and skills in order to stimulate growth.

✓ Be aware of unintentional bias about race, gender, religion, age, disability, sexual preference, or veteran status.

✓ Maintain confidentiality. Assure that disclosure is mutually agreeable when necessary.

✓ Listen and provide counsel, guidance, and suggestions.

✓ Recognize the need to change the relationship; mentor changes may need to occur due to organizational changes, maturity, and other reasons.

✓ Take time to get to know employees. Find out where their interests lie and what skills and abilities they think that they need to develop.

✓ Share your own career experiences to help employees understand the timing and informal processes around promotions or job changes.

✓ Keep employees informed about the strategic direction of the organization and how that may affect their jobs or potential to advance.

Is it worth it? Here again are three first-person testimonials that help attest to the fact that coaching and mentoring are valuable activities for supervisors, managers, and the employees with whom they work.

"I was one of two women on a task force and worked on a daily basis with the most senior employee. I began to have a real appreciation for how people at the top feel about employees. They really want their people to see them as human beings, to be able to have them respond to them that way and to understand their likes, dislikes, desires and abilities, and so on. This experience helped me to be able to deal with the hierarchy in other areas."

"My coach taught me indirectly through business discussions and role modeling."

"I realized I would be a success when I got my first responsible position and handled it on my own. I went to an assignment in a foreign country and had to deal with everything from office location to human resource. It was like running a small company. I was scared stiff, but I did it successfully."

HOW TO SUPERVISE CHALLENGING EMPLOYEES

Hank Karp

Hank Karp, *Ph.D., is principal of Personal Growth Systems (109 82nd St., Virginia Beach, VA 23451, 804-425-8203), a consulting firm specializing in conflict management, leadership and supervisory training, and executive coaching. Hank is the author of* **Personal Power: An Unorthodox Guide to Success** *(Gardner Press, 1995) and* **The Change Leader: Using a Gestalt Approach with Work Groups** *(Pfeiffer & Company, 1995).*

This guide contains useful advice for a supervisor who is faced with employees who are not easy to manage. You will find the advice given to be refreshingly different from most of what you read on the subject.

Supervising employees has become something of an art form in view of today's constantly changing organizational structures. Where 30 years ago there was simply a foreman, today there are project managers, team leaders, and self-directed group facilitators, each title reflecting the structure and nature of the work group. Leadership and supervisory training have made impressive strides in keeping up with these new structures and emerging organizational values. Most current supervisory training places its emphasis on team effort, establishing and maintaining quality standards, and constantly tracking and measuring results.

With managers learning all these new and creative approaches and trainers focusing on larger system interventions, one risk is emerging at the same rate: *the decreased emphasis on and awareness of the fact that, in the final analysis, all supervisory effectiveness occurs between two people, right here, right now.*

This situation is never more evident or more problematic for the supervisor than when the supervisor is faced with the situation of individual workers who simply will not conform to norms or who refuse to render themselves easy to manage. Despite all the new and creative approaches to supervision that are now proliferating, this problem is no less prevalent today than it was 30 years ago.

There is no magic for converting a challenging or difficult employee into a cooperative and productive one. The underlying assumption arising from many current training programs suggests that there is something wrong with the difficult employee. The challenge to the supervisor is to identify the flaw and then proceed to fix the broken worker through the use of various approaches, skills, and strategies.

A different underlying assumption for the problem and an accompanying process for dealing with challenging employees is as follows: The assumption is that there is nothing wrong with the resisting employee; if there is a problem, it lies in our inability as managers, supervisors, and trainers to respond to the ongoing situation appropriately. That is, if we assume that there is something wrong with the "broken" worker and if we don't get the desired outcome we are striving for, then it is not our fault; after all, you know what *those* people are like, *nobody* can do anything with them.

Certainly, at times the fault does lie squarely with the employee. The question is, which initial assumption is it safest to make. If we assume that the basic fault lies in our own present lack of ability to respond, then we can take responsibility for that and change our behavior to respond more appropriately to the situation. It is a lot easier to change my own behavior to get what I want from you than it is to assume that I can change your behavior merely by telling you what I want.

Ten axioms are derived from the second assumption, that is, if there is something wrong, it is with us as managers, supervisors, and trainers, not with the employees themselves. These axioms will help you to take more control in any situation dealing with difficult or inappropriate behavior, regardless to which basic assumption you choose to adhere.

Axiom 1: People will always do what is in their best self-interest.

The single most naive and frequent assumption made by the marginal supervisor is that *"The worker is paid a fair wage and therefore should be counted on to always do what is in the best interest of the organization."* This is like saying, "I paid list price for my car, so it should never need its oil changed."

The bottom line is that people will want what they want, regardless of who says that they should or should not, and that includes themselves. By encouraging an open expression of this, you can benefit three ways. First, you legitimize the worker's right to his or her own preferences. Second, you have an opportunity to link the worker's wants to the group objectives and develop a greater buy-in on the part of the worker. Third, you develop a more supportive working relationship.

Axiom 2: People are not a problem in their own eyes.

One reasonable assumption is that, all things being equal, people would rather be successful than failing, respected than discounted, liked than disliked. When somebody takes an adversarial position with the supervisor or the organization, they do so at great personal cost. A smart question to ask is "What's the person getting that's good out of this?"

While all behavior may not be motivated, all behavior is determined. If you take the time and have the patience to find out what the person wants, you may be able to provide it at little cost to either of you.

Axiom 3: The number one cause for inappropriate behavior is lack of personal recognition.

The one message that nobody will tolerate for long is "You do not exist," and there is ample anecdotal material to support this. For example, experienced social workers will tell you that children often will collude in their own abuse. That is, they will nag the abusive parent until there is a reaction. This startling bit of information supports the point that some kids would rather be hurt than ignored. Adults, in a less dramatic context, are no different. Check out your own reaction to a call not returned, a question elicited but not answered, or being kept waiting for no good reason.

By providing your direct reports with immediate, specific, and behavior-focused feedback on a regular basis, you not only begin to reverse inappropriate behavior, but you can often prevent it from occurring in the first place.

Axiom 4: Your most difficult workers are often your most motivated ones as well.

The natural tendency for many people is to ascribe the worst possible motivation for inappropriate behavior when the underlying reason is not clear. One major cause is that the worker is a lot brighter and more growth-oriented than the work being done requires. The inevitable result is that, once boredom sets in, the worker finds a way to respond to it, through horseplay, goading you, or avoiding the work area as much as possible.

Before castigating the difficult worker for being noncooperative, check out what she or he would rather be doing. Chances are that, if you can increase the opportunity for achievement, recognition for achievement, responsibility, growth, or interest in the work itself, you will be providing a much preferred alternative to the current problem behavior.

Axiom 5: Deal with specific behaviors and their effects, *never* with attitudes.

Anything that is causing a problem is, by definition, a behavior. If you attack someone's attitude, you are making the attack personal. The worker will get defensive at best or counterattack at worst. *Never refer to anyone's attitudes, beliefs, or values in an attempt to get cooperative behavior!*

The simplest and most effective way of dealing with any problematic behavior is to

1. Describe the behavior in specific detail.
2. Show what the specific effects of the behavior are.
3. Provide a reasonable alternative.

> For example, "Charley, you have been tying up the office phone for personal calls. When this happens, customers don't have immediate access to us, which hurts our performance. Unless it's an emergency, I'd like you to hold your personal calls until lunch, when you can use the phone in the break room."

Axiom 6: There is no such thing as a bad human characteristic or capacity.

> Any behavior that is causing you a problem, such as aggressiveness, passivity, or gossiping, could be quite appropriate in another context. Rather than attacking the behavior itself, you will get less resistance to change if you illustrate how the particular behavior was inappropriate in the present circumstances.

Axiom 7: Your primary function is not to make demands. It is to assist the worker in making better choices.

> The truth is that a supervisor cannot make anyone do anything that they really don't want to do. Acknowledging this fact is the easiest way to begin to shape the behavior of the other person. Not only does it put the working relationship on more realistic grounds, but it also acknowledges the power of the other person. Once acknowledged, there is much less need to prove it.
>
> Once you get the employee to see where the current behavior is inappropriate and you are clear about what the other person wants, work toward generating three options, each of which has a probability of resulting in the desired outcome.

Axiom 8: The best way to get a change in the other person's behavior is to make a sudden and unexpected change in your own.

> If you have become used to a specific style of dealing with your direct reports, chances are that they can pretty well anticipate your reaction to the difficult behavior and be ready for it. Try something completely different and see what happens. For example, if you tend toward the gruff, impersonal approach to supervision, try listening and counseling rather than berating the inappropriate employee the next time you have to deal with the behavior.
>
> By the same token, if you are a devotee of the modern approach to supervision and can always be counted on to listen, understand, and be supportive, try an alternative approach. The next time you get a repeat infraction, get in touch with your frustration and express it clearly and appropriately. Then make a clear and unequivocal demand for change.

Axiom 9: Unless you transfer the pain, it remains with you.

There is no reason in the world for the difficult employee to change behavior simply because you or someone else does not like it. After all, you are the person who is having the problem with the behavior, not the employee.

As mentioned earlier, you count on people to do what is in their best self-interest, so it is merely a matter of showing the employee where the best self-interest lies. I am *not* suggesting that you do anything hurtful, only that you use your skills to point out the contingencies for continuing the present behavior. For example, "Charlie, this is your third lateness this month. If it happens again, you could be put on disciplinary probation and neither of us wants that. What can we do to make sure that this doesn't happen?"

Axiom 10: When a condition of inappropriate behavior has existed for two months or longer, there is *always* collusion between you and the employee to keep it that way.

As painful as this sounds, it is also true. The proof of this statement is that if this were not the case you would be doing something differently than you are presently doing in an attempt to change the behavior.

You need to get in touch with what you are getting out of the present situation or what bad thing might happen if the difficult behavior went away. Some examples are that you won't have to risk a direct confrontation, you sort of enjoy the give and take of the present situation, or dealing with the difficult employee is preferable to something you would have to do if he or she were not there.

Once you are clear about the positive aspects of the situation, you can more freely generate a strategy for dealing with it without risking the loss of the positive rewards.

Conclusion

Dealing with difficult employees can be one of the more exciting and challenging aspects of your job as a supervisor, manager, or trainer once you develop the confidence in your ability to do so. There may be additional axioms that are appropriate to your particular situation as well.

Finally, when you are faced with a difficult employee and you don't know what to do, ask yourself these three questions:

1. What am I aware of right now? (*The specific behavior, its effects, and how you feel about the situation.*)

2. What do I want, right now? (*What specific change in behavior do you want? When?*)

3. How am I stopping myself from getting this, right now? (*Fill in the blank, then go for it.*)

HOW TO REVITALIZE EMPLOYEES

Wayne Pace and Douglas McGregor

R. Wayne Pace, *Ph.D., is professor of organizational behavior, Marriott School of Management, Brigham Young University. Dr. Pace has been president of the Academy of Human Resource Development, the International Communication Association, and the Western States Communication Association. He is the author of 15 books and dozens of articles, monographs, and research reports on organizational behavior and communication. Dr. Pace may be contacted about issues of work-force revitalization at 440 East 2320 North, Provo, Utah 84604, 801-374-2870.* **Douglas R. McGregor** *is senior organizational performance technologist, Control Systems Division, Parker Bertea Aerospace, a division of Parker Hannifin Corporation. Doug may be contacted about issues of revitalization at 515 15th Street, Ogden, Utah 84404, 801-392-4002.*

This guide suggests how you can increase employee motivation by appealing to employees' natural growth goals. Five steps are described to implement this unique motivational approach.

Organizations are moving into a new era of competitiveness. To compete, organizations must improve two subsystems:

1. The *technical,* which involves business process reengineering to achieve immediacy in the production and delivery of products and services

2. The *social,* which involves revitalizing or generating high levels of motivation in employees so that they can achieve immediacy in the production and delivery of products and services (see Taylor and Felten, 1993)

A major way to revitalize employees that is described in this guide is accomplished through the process of identifying and achieving *natural growth goals* (Garfield, 1986). Natural growth goals (NGGs) are conscious intentions of individuals to achieve some purposeful action that allows them to learn, grow, and expand in their lives. Gardner (1963) attests to the power of natural growth goals when he writes that "everyone has noted the astonishing sources of energy that seem available to those who enjoy what they are doing or find meaning in what they are doing" (p. 16).

We have identified 12 natural growth goals.

1. To work at one's highest potential in a specific area of expertise
2. To use all of one's capacities to develop excellence in several areas of knowledge and skill
3. To explore new opportunities and new ways of doing things
4. To be a prime mover by initiating new ideas and influencing others
5. To be totally involved in a project and reluctant to let others down
6. To contribute to the well-being of others
7. To have one's efforts add up to something meaningful
8. To be free to make responsible and independent decisions
9. To do things in one's unique, personal, and individual way
10. To have high aspirations for doing more than what seems possible
11. To respond optimistically and with pleasure and pride in what others accomplish
12. To envision the possibilities of future accomplishments

There is good evidence that these natural growth goals energize and direct behavior (Locke and Latham, 1990, pp. 1–16). In the workplace, individuals are often faced with a wide variety of competing tasks. They organize their time and energy by focusing on some tasks while ignoring others. One way to regulate behavior is through goal setting.

Natural growth goals are the ideas, aims, and purposes that direct and give intensity and persistence to actions that result in people becoming greater than they were before the actions. The achievement of natural growth goals results in the expansion and development of people. Blockage of natural growth goals, however, leads to the diminishing and shrinking of people. Continual learning—both individual and organizational—is central to achieving natural growth goals and having the vitality to be competitive in this new era.

The Process of Revitalization through Natural Growth Goals

1. *Select several moderately difficult goals that are challenging to achieve, but that when accomplished will give success experiences early.* Look over the preceding list of 12 natural growth goals and select one that is relevant to the employees in your organization. For example, consider NGG number 1—*to work at one's highest potential in a specific area of expertise.* Next, brainstorm some tentative ideas for how employees in the organization could achieve this goal. Make a tentative decision on the following scale about how difficult and challenging the goal will be to accomplish and another tentative decision about the likelihood of having early successes in achieving the goal.

	Idea					
Very easy to achieve	1	2	3	4	5	Very difficult to achieve
Unlikely to get early success	1	2	3	4	5	Very likely to get early success

Study the list of natural growth goals and select another, such as NGG number 8—*to do things in one's unique, personal, and individual way*. Now, brainstorm again some tentative ideas for what could be done to change organization processes so that employees could achieve this goal. After looking over the list of things that might need to be done, make a tentative decision about how difficult and challenging it will be for employees to accomplish the goal and another decision about the likelihood of having early successes in achieving the goal.

	Idea					
Very easy to achieve	1	2	3	4	5	Very difficult to achieve
Unlikely to get early success	1	2	3	4	5	Very likely to get early success

Continue to identify natural growth goals to achieve and to brainstorm ways in which organization members could achieve the goals. Continue to evaluate the difficulty of achieving the goals and the likelihood of getting early successes.

As soon as you feel that all the relevant and appropriate natural growth goals have been identified and evaluated, proceed to select the three to six goals to be implemented as part of this process. As a goal is selected, place the goal at the top of a new page and list the tentative ideas resulting from the brainstorming. Continue until each goal is listed on a separate page with the appropriate ideas.

Proceed to step 2.

2. *Identify programs and activities for each goal that could be used to achieve the goal.* Take the page for the first goal to be achieved and study the tentative ideas for similarities. Mark the goals that fit together with different symbols for easy identification. Add new ideas as they occur to you and mark them appropriately. Continue through the list of tentative ideas until all ideas listed have been grouped and all additional ideas have been grouped.

Now, take the first group of ideas and give it a programmatic name. For example, ideas associated with the goal to work at one's highest potential might have a cluster of ideas that all involve acquiring additional skills. These might be called a program for "starting a training program." Proceed to the next group of ideas and give it a programmatic name.

Continue by making certain that the program and activities are both related to one another, but somewhat independent of each other. This is sometimes a difficult paradox to overcome, but to be successful it is important that the program and activities do not overlap and, at the same time, that they complement one another. For example, a plant beautification program would be independent of a series of open houses, but they would complement one another.

Complete the process of identifying programs and activities to achieve each goal, measuring the ideas for independence and complementarity each time, until all the goals have a complete package of programs and activities.

3. *Make certain that the programs and activities are consistent with the culture of the organization.* So far we have been concerned primarily with the identification of individual natural development goals and the creation of programs and activities to achieve those goals to enhance individual vigor and enthusiasm. To sustain the energy and vitality generated by the potential achievement of these goals, we must make certain that the programs and activities are consistent with and supportive of the culture of the organization. This step in the process requires everyone involved to reflect on what is important and acceptable to both employees and the organization as a whole and together to assess the extent to which the programs and activities will contribute to and avoid conflict with the culture of the organization and support, or at least not conflict with, the basic cultural assumptions of the organization.

The culture consists of things, sayings, doings, and feelings shared by members of the organization. Together, the objects, talk, behavior, and emotions shared by organization members determine what is acceptable to do in an organization. For example, in a high-tech manufacturing business the culture may be such that it is difficult to implement an after-hours fine arts program to allow employees to express themselves in painting, sculpting, and classical music or to sponsor a company golf team. Although such activities and programs might find acceptance in another context, in this organization, as desirable as they might be, they would just conflict with the culture.

Conflicts with the culture of an organization are part of almost all change projects. In some cases, the achievement of some natural growth goals are in and of themselves culture change interventions. However, in this example, to be successful, programs and activities would need to be compatible with the ongoing culture of the organization.

4. *Prepare specific action plans to implement the programs and activities that will lead to achieving the natural growth goals.* This step in the process of implementing natural growth goals involves stating the actions in relatively concrete sets of behavioral sequences that can be carried out to achieve each goal.

A concrete behavioral sequence simply specifies what is to be done, one action after another. For example, implementing a leadership training program in an organization using distance learning or training that is brought into the organization from a trainer who is off site might involve the following steps:

   a. The manager of human resource development appoints a coordinator of distant training.

   b. The coordinator contacts a local college or university that offers closed-circuit courses and has distance learning facilities to teach a leadership course over closed–circuit television from its campus to the training facilities of the company.

   c. The coordinator works with engineering to install closed-circuit television facilities so as to receive the course on site.

   d. The coordinator assists in the selection of a trainer.

   e. The coordinator helps design the training program and how it will be facilitated.

   f. The coordinator and the human resource development manager decide how often the course will be offered.

5. *Provide confirmation of success in achieving the natural growth goals.* Confirmation is a better term to use in this context than rewards, since the term rewards connotes an act to trigger behavior. Here we are concerned about communicating to the organization members that their work has been confirmed and that they have been successful in achieving the natural growth goals and carrying out the plans and programs. Achievement of the goals is the reward. Organization members, however, seek confirmation that what they are doing is acceptable.

Most reward programs are in fact simply confirmations anyway. Traditional awards, such as letters of commendation, plaques, certificates, and coupons or cash payments, are, literally, not rewards; they are more accurately thought of as confirmations. That is, the plaques indicate to employees that what they have been doing is acceptable, consistent with the culture of the organization, and thus valued by the organization. Nevertheless, it is important to provide confirmation. One vitalizing program that organizations should consider is just that of confirming on a regular basis the accomplishments of organization members.

Growth is the human process of expanding and developing; growth results from continuous learning and maturing. Thus, developing, learning, and maturing are interrelated concepts that encompass the sense of growth. Through growth, individuals become stronger, more dependable, more accomplished, more competent, happier, more autonomous, more influential, more emotionally stable, and more adaptive.

There is good evidence that goals energize and direct behavior. In fact, we assume that all of life's aspirations are shaped by a series of goals that lead us to progressively higher levels of achievement. Natural growth goals are strengthened through their regular achievement. Vitality in the workplace depends to a great extent on developing natural growth goals. This emphasis on growth and learning in the workplace may be unique in our time, or, possibly, it may be that it has just become more important to us at this time. In any case, we must seriously use natural growth goals to enhance the learning, growth, and vitality of the work force.

REFERENCES

Gardner, John. 1963. *Self-renewal.* New York: Harper & Row.

Garfield, Charles. 1986. "Understanding Growth," *Peak Performers.* New York: Avon Books, 57–58.

Hackman, J. Richard, and Greg H. Oldham. 1980. *Work Redesign.* Reading, MA: Addison-Wesley Publishing Co.

Locke, Edwin A., and Gary P. Latham. 1990. *A theory of Goal Setting & Task Performance.* Upper Saddle River, NJ: Prentice Hall, 1–26.

Miller, Donald B. 1977. *Personal Vitality.* Reading, MA: Addison-Wesley Publishing Co.

Taylor, James C., and David F. Felton. 1993. *Performance by Design.* Upper Saddle River, NJ: Prentice Hall.

HOW TO STRUCTURE
LONG-DISTANCE MENTORING

34

George Piskurich

George M. Piskurich, *Ph.D., is a consultant in training systems and instructional design (102 Fernwood Court, Chapel Hill, NC 27516, 919-968-0878). He has been in the training profession in various industry settings for over 20 years. His areas of special interest include self-directed learning, instructional design and technology, and management development. He has written extensively, presented at national and international conferences on topics from mentoring systems to customer service, and served in many capacities for the American Society for Training and Development (ASTD) and the National Society for Performance and Instruction (NSPI).*

Training in companies that have a significant number of sites can be difficult to accomplish in a timely and cost-efficient manner. Imagine that you are given the task of designing a training program for one such company. How would you handle the situation? This guide details how one organization, with sites scattered throughout much of the country, used a structured mentoring approach to solve the problems of distance, constant organizational change, and the need for "just-in-time" training. Included at the end of this guide is a list of questions to ask yourself before you select a similar approach for your situation.

Start with 2000 training sites in 28 states, add a turnover rate of roughly 60% for the intended audience, blend in the 12 trainers currently available to do the training, and stir well with a brand new management team that is changing policy and procedures faster than they can be updated in the manuals. What you end up with is a concoction guaranteed to put even the best training department "under the table" with one sip.

These characteristics were only part of the problem facing a large retail company in their management training program. The need was to provide new managers at the chains 2000 stores with the information that they needed to run a $2 to $3 million profit center virtually on their own. The audience ranged from highly experienced professionals hired from other companies, who of course knew the "right" way to do everything, to recent college graduates who were not sure of the way to do anything in the off-campus environment. The previous training program consisted of giving the new manager the keys and asking him to "keep the store open and the product from walking out."

Because of the turnover situation and the absolute need for "some kind" of manager in each store, new hires began any day of the week, anywhere in the company's 28-state area. Once in the stores, it was almost impossible to get the managers out again for training classes. Their supervisors controlled anywhere between 15 and 30 stores in what could be up to a three-state area. Supervision was minimal and the use of supervisors as trainers unreliable at best.

The material was basically "how to manage a store," including store policy and procedures, finance and accounting, company personnel and general policy and procedures, and basic supervision for those new to the process. The goal was to turn the new hire into a store manager who knew, and more importantly practiced, store management the way the company wanted it practiced.

There was another significant problem. Due to management team changes, the way the company wanted a store to be managed changed almost daily. This included not only policy and procedural changes, but also what was expected of the manager as far as increased supervisory and higher-level management responsibilities were concerned.

The training department had already begun a self-directed learning design for the training of store employees, but SDL takes time to develop. The need here was too critical, and the material changed too fast to make SDL a viable design. Other highly time-intensive designs such as computer-based training or multimedia would also be too slow and were thus eliminated from consideration.

Classroom formats were obviously out of the question, for many of the reasons described earlier. This left on-the-job training, or some modification of an OJT process, as the only design category that held any promise. However, the stores were relatively small and short staffed. There was no one in most of them to be the OJT facilitator, even if he or she had the ability, which most did not (remember the phrase "here's the key, don't let the product walk out").

The Structured Mentoring System

The design decided on was a modified OJT process in which mentors were developed at stores within each geographic district. These stores became *training stores* in which new managers could spend part or all of their day learning what they needed to know and do. They would then practice these new skills and knowledges back at their own stores.

However, it was not the store, but the manager of the store, that made the system work. Each *manager mentor* was handpicked by the district supervisor as having the best combination of expertise, willingness, and time to be a mentor. The supervisor was assisted in this task by a mentor characteristics checklist provided by the training department.

To provide structure for the process, the mentors were given a mentor guide and a trainee guide that they could use during the training. The mentor guide was developed from an intense job analysis in which a number of the soon to be mentors and their managers participated in focus groups to determine the exact tasks a new manager had to master. These tasks were converted into objectives, and the objectives were in turn converted into the mentor guide.

A special aspect of these focus groups was that the participants were also asked to share their methods for managing stores, what tricks they used, what special forms they had developed on their own, and what they found that worked and did not work. These ideas were incorporated into the mentor guide under the relevant objectives so that each mentor could use them as they trained new store managers. Other references, appropriate readings, and supplementary material, all categorized by objective, completed the mentor guide.

The trainee guide included the objectives and any forms, data, or information that would be directly relevant to them. It also included a series of self-quizzes based on each objective and its accompanying supporting objectives. The trainees could complete these quizzes to check on their progress and then discuss them with their mentor. This lent a somewhat self-directed component to the training without the need to develop labor-intensive self-directed programming. The final program consisted of 32 program objectives with over 100 supporting objectives, covering in detail everything needed to be a store manager.

The mentors were trained in the use of the materials through a series of learning sessions conducted throughout the company. The regional supervisors (the mentors' bosses) were also trained in how the program would work and were given their own guide that detailed their responsibilities. To keep them directly involved, the design included objectives that were the regional supervisor's responsibility to teach. This gave them more than just an administrative interest in the program. Included in the training classes at both levels was a heavy dose of information on how to train, particularly in a one-on-one format. Because mentors and supervisors changed, often with little notice, the class information was later developed as a self-directed learning package. This allowed new mentors to begin their responsibilities without waiting for an explanatory class.

To complete the process, guidelines were developed on when and how the training should be done. This included a schedule of how long each objective should take to complete, how the objectives should be sequenced, and the inevitable forms for beginning and ending the process. There were also monthly progress reports, checklists, and, at the urging of some more strongly left brained vice-presidents, a final written examination. (Actually, in the first evaluation of the program the graduates felt the exam to be of great value. It continued to remain part of the program, and a performance component was added to make it more reflective of what the trainees were really learning and responsible for.) Certificates and program evaluations completed by trainees, mentors, and district supervisors added the finishing touches to the program.

This system was designed to deal with the problem of constantly changing policy and procedures by having the real information reside in the minds of the mentors. Therefore, getting updates and changes to the mentors was critical. This was handled through a special mentor's newsletter and twice-a-year meetings where in-depth information concerning current and planned procedural changes was discussed with mentors and district supervisors. Not missing a chance to polish mentoring skills, the training department provided mentoring tips for the newsletter and continuing train-the-trainer materials during the meetings.

To follow up and reinforce the training, the new managers were visited at their store by their mentor from time to time during the year after they completed the program. In these visits special problems of this particular store could be discussed, and the mentor looked for indicators of other problems or weaknesses that the new manager needed to work on. The performance portion of the final test was practiced during the first of these visits, and when the mentor felt the new manager was ready, the district supervisor visited the store to administer both the written and performance areas of the test.

The Results

The results of the implementation were very positive. From a rather simplistic, though nonetheless important point of view, an average of 40 individuals a month, who would have taken over the management of a store with practically no knowledge of what they were to do, were trained to "do it right." Formal program evaluations from all levels of the organization were consistently high. The mastery level of 80% on the final test was met by over 90% of the trainees on the first try. Those who did not achieve mastery continued in the program and were retested.

Follow-up interviews done at the training stores and in the new store managers' stores were overwhelmingly positive. Managers experienced with other chains commented routinely that this was the best training system that they had ever experienced. While certainly a response to more variables than training, turnover was reduced to less than 20% for store managers, and store profits increased each reporting period that the training system was in place.

The program was so well received that the objectives and materials were reformatted into a quasi-self-directed learning package that store managers who had not attended the program could use to analyze their comprehension of the company's way to manage a store. Their analysis was shared with their supervisors, and they were given opportunities to obtain help in areas where they found themselves lacking.

Perhaps the most important lesson learned was that flexibility is the key to a structured mentoring system. When the first edition of the program was distributed, it was highly structured. Schedules for training, sequencing, lengths of time for completion, testing, and exact expectations for who would do what, when, and where were all part of the process. Preliminary evaluation found that many mentors and their supervisors could not deal with such regimentation due to geographic and business-related variables. The second edition was much more free form, with more recommendations and less formality. Unfortunately, a number of the experienced mentors who received the "new and improved" guide complained about the lack of structure, because we took away their schedules and checklists. The answer was to provide structure, even overstructure, but to make only key aspects mandatory, such as the final examination and a midway progress report. Other than these requirements, the message given to the mentors and supervisors was that the trainees must master the objectives. It was their call as to how and in what sequence and timing this occurred.

Even the paper work became flexible as some regions of the company developed their own systems for record keeping and evaluation. It was difficult for the instructional designers at headquarters who had crafted all the pieces so carefully into the "perfect" design to let go and allow the program to truly reflect the highly decentralized nature of the company. However, over time the program became regionalized and, for the most part, as decentralized as the company itself. Mastering the objectives was the only headquarters imperative. That never changed, although the objectives surely did, practically each time an evaluation was done for a new edition.

A second lesson was that there are some things still best taught in a classroom and much to be gained from having the trainees meet and share their experiences and ideas. Toward this end, a three-day classroom experience was added to the mentoring program. Here subjects such as personnel issues, supervisory skills, and current corporate philosophy and strategic planning were discussed by corporate experts. There was plenty of time built in for idea exchange both formally in the class and informally at dinners and an outing.

The class developed such a good reputation that experienced managers began to ask for inclusion, complaining that their new colleagues were learning things that they didn't know about. Instead of running special classes for the old-timers, these managers were blended a few at a time into the new manager classes, thus adding their experiences and knowledge to the mix. A mistake that was made, though, was to make it mandatory for old-time managers to attend the class. It was quickly realized that this only created problems, both in the class and back in the store.

A third lesson was not new but seems to always need to be relearned—communication. In this program there was no such thing as too much of it. Mentors needed to be constantly updated as did the trainees. Supervisors needed help in picking the right mentors and efficient ways of communicating changes in mentors or training stores when a mentor was reassigned. Administration needed to know if there were problems with the program in a district, because this invariably meant bigger problems in the district as a whole. This required stronger communications from the mentors to the corporate level than first designed. As the program became more regionally oriented, information from the field about changes and how they were working needed to be communicated to the corporate level as well. If the changes were generally useful and applicable, they were communicated back to other field areas.

This all required people who were paying attention to the process on an ongoing basis and turned into an almost full-time job for the 12 field trainers mentioned at the beginning of this guide. They may have been too few to teach, but they could be the backbone of communications throughout the program and the company. In large structured mentoring systems such as this, field coordinators are an integral part of the communications process.

In the final analysis, a structured mentoring system designed for this particular environment is basically a distance learning process. It has all the advantages and disadvantages of any distance learning design. It requires flexible structure, careful selection and training of the right mentors, the provision of good, useful materials, continuous communications, listening skills, evaluations and revisions, and the supply of both the mentors and the trainees with what they tell you they need to succeed.

When the structured mentoring program began, the company involved had just declared a Chapter 11 bankruptcy. Three years later a healthy, profitable company emerged from Chapter 11 and is still growing and succeeding today. A good instructional design, which effectively and efficiently trained the people most directly responsible for making money for the company, played no small part in this success.

Is a long-distance structured mentoring program appropriate for your company? Use the following checklist to determine when this approach is appropriate.

10 QUESTIONS TO ASK BEFORE CHOOSING STRUCTURED MENTORING

If you can answer yes *to most of these questions, structured mentoring is appropriate for your organization or training need.*

1. Is standardization (consistency) of learning important?

2. Do you have many different training sites and few instructors?

3. Do you have high turnover or many new hires?

4. Do you need to have the trainees learning at their own pace due to individual differences?

5. Do you have a need for "just-in-time" training?

6. Do you have to keep repeating the same classes over and over again?

7. Are you spending too much on bringing trainees to your programs?

8. Do your development programs produce more individualized needs than you can handle?

9. Are your participants complaining that they cannot make your scheduled classes?

10. Will the cost (in both money and time) of SDL development be cheaper than the long-term cost of implementing a stand-up program?

HOW TO REENGINEER YOUR LIFE*

Bonnie Michaels

Bonnie Michaels *is president of Managing Work & Family, Inc. (912 Crain St., Evanston, IL 60202, 708-864-0916), a work–family consulting and training firm. Bonnie is an internationally recognized work–family consultant and coauthor of* **Solving the Work/Family Puzzle** *(Business One, Irwin, 1992). A keynote speaker and contributor to major publications, Bonnie works with corporations to identify and analyze work–family needs and then develop long-term strategies with effective internal programs, policies, and services.*

This step-by-step guide offers you an opportunity to embark on a journey of self-discovery as you proceed sequentially through the creation of a **whole life plan.** *The eight-step guide includes a self-assessment instrument that assists you in finding a better balance between your work and personal lives. The whole life plan can be used by human resource professionals and trainers as part of larger stress-management and career-development workshops or by individuals who are simply interested in achieving a more balanced life-style.*

Do you feel as though your life is out of control? Are you often exhausted, depressed, and angry? Do you feel like you never have enough time for your personal life? Individuals who have these symptoms often feel that they don't have any choices as to how they spend their time. By stepping back and analyzing what is actually going on in your life, you can begin a process of creating a plan for a life with balance. The following eight steps will assist you in the development of a plan to reengineer your life and bring it back into balance.

1. *Assess your current life situation.* If you feel out of balance, either because there is too much on your plate, too little, or an unsatisfying mix, identify where the dissatisfaction comes from. Try using the following life satisfaction index.

*How to Reengineer Your Life was adapted from Bonnie Michaels and Elizabeth McCarty, Solving the Work/Family Puzzle, Business One, Irwin, 1992.

My Life Satisfaction Index

Circle your response to the following statements. "Enough time" means the amount of time necessary for you to feel satisfied.

		Never	Rarely	Sometimes	Often	Always
1. a.	I spend enough time with my spouse or partner; or	1	2	3	4	5
b.	I want a spouse or partner and am actively looking for one.	1	2	3	4	5
2.	I spend enough time with my children.	1	2	3	4	5
3.	I spend enough time with my elders.	1	2	3	4	5
4.	I spend enough time with my friends.	1	2	3	4	5
5.	My career does not interfere with my personal life.	1	2	3	4	5
6.	I make time for spiritual growth.	1	2	3	4	5
7.	I am satisfied with my physical condition.	1	2	3	4	5
8.	I spend enough time on my own intellectual stimulation.	1	2	3	4	5
9.	I spend enough time alone or doing things just for me.	1	2	3	4	5
10.	I am generally happy.	1	2	3	4	5
11.	I enjoy my work.	1	2	3	4	5
12.	My personal life does not interfere with my work.	1	2	3	4	5
13.	I experience joy in my accomplishments, my relationships, my children.	1	2	3	4	5

Now add up your points and look at where you stand overall.

46–60	You are pretty happy with the way things are. Read on if you would like to make life even better.
31–45	You are satisfied more than not. As you read, pay close attention to those areas where your satisfaction level is low.
15–30	Tired of feeling so-so? Take charge and replan!
0–15	Time for a major overhaul.

2. *Examine your values.* To establish a successful whole life plan, it is important to take a look at your values and desires related to your work and personal life. Family and cultural values are the belief system with which we were raised. They often relate to how people should behave, how they should interact, and what they should do. Instead of acting on "shoulds," ask yourself "What is really important?"

Values

_____

_____

_____

3. *Set new goals.* Whole life planning means setting goals for the whole person—social, intellectual, spiritual, and physical. It means striving to achieve balance and harmony in all areas by setting realistic goals and reaching them. Start now by listing the five things you would most like to accomplish in each area. Don't eliminate those things you think you couldn't or shouldn't do. Dare to dream.

_____

_____

_____

_____

_____

4. *Set a family plan.* None of us lives in a vacuum. If you are married or living with someone, the values, goals, and priorities of your partner play a major role in your ability to accomplish your goals. Other family members also affect us. Ask your partner, or anyone else who plays a major part in your personal life, to also do a values clarification exercise and identify his or her own goals. Then discuss each of your goals and priorities, how conflicts can be resolved, and how you can help each other to achieve your goals. Be honest about what you and your partner want from careers and family life.

Self-Goals

_____

_____

_____

_____

_____

Family Goals

_____

_____

_____

_____

For each goal you have identified, ask yourself the following questions.

Is my goal specific, measurable, and clearly defined?

Is my goal flexible (do alternatives exist)?

Is my goal something *I* want (not what others want for me)?

Is my goal possible (within my physical, mental, and emotional abilities)?

Is my goal powerful, representing something I feel passionate about?

Is my goal big enough?

If you answered *no* for any goal, rephrase or replace it with a goal that meets these criteria.

5. *Share your goals.* By verbalizing the goal and making it public with other family and friends, you acknowledge it to yourself as well as others and get support. Others will help you and provide resources in ways that you could never predict.

6. *Develop an action plan.* Identify the actions you need to take to achieve each of your goals. What do you need to do to accomplish your goals? Do you need to take classes, have more time for yourself? What would it take? Use another sheet if you need more room. Leave the time frames blank for now.

Action Plan

	Goals	*Actions*
1.	_____	_____
2.	_____	_____
3.	_____	_____
4.	_____	_____
5.	_____	_____

7. *Look at the big picture.* It is important to look at the big picture when you create a whole life plan to help you to realize that life is (hopefully) long. There may be many opportunities for you to reach your goals. In setting time frames for your action plan and goals, also consider how the three sets of goals interrelate. Which goals can you do at once and which may be more appropriately pursued late in your life? Delaying some goals while you work on others is often referred to as *sequencing.*

8. *Set goals over time.* Now let's prioritize the goals over time. Go back to your Action Plan and decide on the time elements (1 month, six months, 1 year, 3 years, 10 years). You can now translate your actions and goals into a whole life plan. Use the chart that follows, *My Whole Life Plan,* or devise one of your own.

9. *Assess your plan.* Every once in a while, pull out your plan. Have you achieved your short-term goals? If yes, give yourself credit and revel in the accomplishments. If not, figure out what went wrong. Did it turn out to be something you did not really want? Did another goal preempt it? Do you want to build it into a later stage? If you are serious about living a conscious life, take the time every year to do another set of short-term goals for the coming year. What new goals can you add? Which old goals can you reaffirm? Take control and do what you want to do with your whole life. It is yours—and it is the only one you have.

Time Frame	Goal*	Action
1 month		
6 months		
1 year		
2 years		
3 years		
4 years		
5 years		
6 years		
7 years		

*Goal: Work goal 1 = WG1; family goal 3 = FG3; self-goal 2 = SG2.

Figure 35.1. My Whole Life Plan.

Time Frame	Goal*	Action
8 years		
9 years		
10 years		
15 years		
20 years		
25 years		
30 years		
50 years		

*Goal: Work goal 1 = WG1; family goal 3 = FG3; self-goal 2 = SG2.

Figure 35.1. *(continued)*

HOW TO INFORMALLY RESOLVE A SEXUAL HARASSMENT COMPLAINT

David McNichol

David McNichol, *Ed.D., is an assistant director of human resource development at Temple University (3333 North Broad St., GSB Room 100, Philadelphia, PA 19140, 215-707-8304). Dave has conducted training and development programs in a wide variety of areas, including supervisory and executive development, team building, quality service, continuous quality improvement, stress management, planning, problem solving, diversity at work (including sexual harassment awareness), and smoking cessation.*

Almost every company has a formal policy for handling sexual harassment complaints within their organization. However, employees are often reluctant to draw attention to themselves through the process of complaining about offensive behaviors that are sexual in nature. This is particularly true when the alleged harasser has management responsibility for the complainant. For this reason, many companies have begun to institute procedures for informally resolving sexual harassment complaints. The following guide details how you can diplomatically handle conversations with first the complainant and then the alleged harasser in this potentially difficult situation.

An informal process for handling sexual harassment complaints allows you as a manager or as a human resource staff member to resolve charges of harassment in a timely and confidential manner. This process is not intended to be used for major violations of your organization's legal sexual harassment policy. Instead, the informal process is similar to an out-of-court arbitration settlement in which both parties have the opportunity to be heard and an agreeable solution is decided on by both the complainant and the alleged harasser.

There are times when it may be inappropriate for you to handle an informal complaint. Perhaps the person being complained about is a friend of yours, or there is an appearance of a conflict of interest. In these situations it may be better for you to explain that you see a conflict of interest and suggest that the complainant meet with another manager or human resource officer who is trained to handle sexual harassment complaints.

The informal process may begin in any number of ways: a phone call, a letter, or a face-to-face discussion. What matters most is not how you first learn of the complaint, but how you deal with the information once you have it. Here are specific suggestions to follow when you have been made aware that a sexual harassment complaint exists.

Handling an Initial Contact or Interview
with a Complainant

1. *Consider privacy first and foremost.* The employee may be reluctant to complain about the behavior of others for fear of retaliation or for fear that they will be viewed as a troublemaker. Encourage employees who call on the phone not to discuss their situation unless they have complete privacy. In-person interviews afford the highest degree of privacy for the complainant. Consider where your desk or office is located. Is it in a high-traffic area? Is it in an open work area where others can hear the discussion? If necessary, reserve private space and forward your incoming calls so that there are no distractions.

2. *Listen with empathy. Your verbal and nonverbal cues should say, "I hear what you are saying and I empathize with your dilemma."* Complainants will be in various emotional states. Fear and anger are two that are often expressed. Depending on the employees' situation, they may tell you a lot or only a little. The key is to let them talk without interrupting. You may be the first person they have spoken to, and they may need to release their tension by venting to you. Nodding your head and letting them know verbally that you hear them helps. Resist the urge to interrupt until a natural break occurs. Say things like "I can understand why that would bother you." Avoid the temptation to say "I know how you feel."

3. *Explain your role to them as soon as you can. They may not have any idea of what you can do to assist them.* As soon as possible, let the employee know that your role is to listen, answer questions, provide information, and assist in *his or her* attempts to informally resolve the situation. Make sure the employee knows that your job is *not* to conduct a formal investigation to determine if the organizational policy prohibiting sexual harassment has been violated.

4. *Make sure that you keep your conversations confidential.* Complainants must believe that their complaints will be handled in strict confidence. This is particularly important when you first meet or speak with a complainant. Know your organization's policy related to confidentiality. Occasionally, a situation is so serious that the organization must take action, usually to protect others, without the consent of the complainant. If this is the case, then let the complainant know that it is possible that confidence will be broken. Often the complainant is the one to break confidentiality. Encourage complainants to be very careful about discussing their situations. The more people told, the more likely that privacy will not be kept. Therefore, "keep the circle small." Depending on the situation, managers may not need to be involved.

5. *Keep specific notes.* Inform the complainant right away if you plan to take notes during your conversations. A complainant may not like the idea of notes, so be flexible about this. Tape recording the discussion is inappropriate. Notes can be taken either during the discussion or immediately afterward. How much detail is needed depends on the situation. Some information is not important at all, while other information may be vital. Always be very sure about names, dates, and times to avoid a mistake in identifying the alleged harasser.

6. *Find out what the complainant wants done about the situation. You may or may not be able to do what he or she is requesting.* Complainants may want to be transferred or they may want the alleged harasser fired. It is unlikely that you will be able to do either of these. Remind them that your job is not to investigate and issue sanctions. Explain the informal resolution options open to them according to your policy. Some of the basic ones usually are the following:

   a. Helping complainants to practice assertively telling the alleged harasser that they resent their unwanted attention

   b. Sending a certified letter in the mail to the alleged harasser stating clearly what the problem is and what the complainant wants to happen in the future

   c. Giving a unit training session that explains what sexual harassment is and the consequences of policy violations (This is not very practical in a small unit.)

   d. Meeting with the alleged harasser and the complainant (provided that this is permitted within your organization's informal resolution process)

   e. Meeting with the alleged harasser, with permission, to communicate the complainant's view of the situation and to reach a possible resolution (To execute this last option you must be absolutely sure that you have the complainant's permission to go forward on his or her behalf.)

7. *Close out the discussion with a summary of what you have learned and, if appropriate, schedule to meet again.* Review the information that you have gathered with the complainant. Check to make sure you have all the pertinent information, that it is accurate, and that there is agreement about what the complainant and you will do next. Find out what is the safest way to contact the complainant, again keeping in mind the importance of confidentiality.

Recognize that the preceding suggestions do not have to occur one after the other. Let the needs of the complainant drive the sequence. However, try to incorporate all these suggestions into the initial interview or contact, and repeat them in future contacts or interviews with the same complainant if necessary. Treat each complainant's case, no matter how similar to another, as separate and unique, because each case is.

Meeting with the Alleged Harasser

Meeting with the alleged harasser can be especially difficult, because your role is to try to informally resolve a problem that he or she may not think exists. The individual may deny that anything ever happened. Expect defensiveness, resentment, and anger. It is also possible that the complainant has falsely accused the alleged harasser for personal reasons. Research suggests that this is rare, but it is still a possibility. Remember, your job is not to investigate the case, but to try to get a resolution of the complainant's charge.

You may need to contact the supervisor of the alleged harasser in order to get permission for him or her to meet with you or to leave his or her area. This all depends on the culture of the organization and on the job level of the alleged harasser. Some hourly staff must account for where they are at all times, so be aware of this and follow appropriate channels. However, it is important to "keep the circle small" and only include those managers that need to know. Find a private place where you can meet and where you will not be interrupted. Avoid the trappings of a formal meeting. Informal resolution should look and sound informal. An alleged harasser may be in a union. If so, request that a union delegate sit in on the meeting, and let the complainant know about this development.

Keep the following suggestions in mind as you meet with the alleged harasser.

1. *Open the meeting with introductions and explain the purpose of the meeting.* The alleged harasser may or may not know exactly why he or she is meeting with you. Explain that you have received a complaint about his or her behavior. Usually, but not always, the complainant has given you permission to use his or her name. If this is so, then tell the alleged harasser who has complained and the nature of the com-

plaint. If you do not have permission to use the complainant's name, just state that you have received a complaint but are not at liberty to reveal a specific name.

If you *do not have permission* to use the complainant's name, provide only some basic general details and not all the specifics. This is not easy to do and from the alleged harasser's perspective may appear unfair. However, the meeting is not a hearing, and you are not trying to determine guilt or innocence. You are a conduit of information for someone else. Just explain that his or her name was mentioned regarding a situation of a sexual or gender nature and that a complainant has come forward and asked you to inform the person that the reported behavior (for example, a touch or degrading comments about men or women) was unwanted or offensive or both.

When you *have permission* to use the complainant's name, provide the alleged harasser with the details that you have been given. Provide as much detail as seems appropriate. However, do not get bogged down in discussing details. Some of the information you received from the complainant may not be completely accurate. Remember that you are not investigating; instead, you are there to communicate the overall concern (someone is offended by someone else's behavior). You want to work out a resolution, not debate details.

2. *Explain your role and the benefits of the informal resolution process.* Let the alleged harasser know as soon as possible that you are not an investigator and that the informal process has been chosen (at this time) by the complainant in lieu of a formal charge, which, depending on the organization's policy, may be used at a future time. Explain that this benefits both the complainant and the alleged harasser because, when a problem situation is worked out informally, it is a win–win situation for all concerned. No disciplinary action should result from an informal intervention and no official paperwork should go into the alleged harasser's personnel file. Again, organizational policies decide these matters, not the person designated to informally resolve the situation.

3. *Listen to his or her side of the story. This is a basic tenet of all counseling situations and is only fair. No two people see the same thing exactly the same way.* You can bet that alleged harassers will see the situation differently from complainants, even if they agree that something happened. Spend some time listening to their side of the story. Like the complainant, they too may want to vent. They may say that the process is unfair, they didn't mean anything by what they did, that nothing of the sort ever happened, and so on. Do not debate with them; just listen and, if appropriate, take notes (you can also do this after the meeting). Let them take notes as well if they consider that necessary. But remember your goal. You want alleged harassers to be

made aware of the situation and that now someone else knows about it and is telling them that it must stop. At this point, they may have questions about the policy and what constitutes sexual harassment. Give them a copy of the policy and take the time to answer their questions. This is all part of the process. If they learn something, then they are moving in the right direction.

4. *Explain what the complainant wants and try to get agreement, if possible.* Tell the alleged harasser what the complainant wants. This may be something very specific, like an apology, or just that the offensive behavior or unwanted attention stop. Details may be important here depending on the nature of the complaint. If it is about language, try to give examples of how words can be offensive. If it is about touch, make it clear that the person should avoid contact with co-workers. Try to get him or her to see how these kinds of behaviors may be viewed by others. Be firm and again do not get bogged down into a debate over details or political correctness. Remind the person that future complaints may result in a formal investigation. Also remind the person about confidentiality and retaliation. Make the alleged harasser aware of the importance of confidentiality. Stress that it is in his or her own best interest and that of the complainant to keep discussions confidential. Assure the person that you intend to do this, too. Exceptions might be if you inform managers, who have already been involved, of the fact that the meeting occurred and that they, as managers, should keep a closer watch on the behavior of the alleged harasser as it relates to sexually harassing. Close the meeting by explaining to the alleged harasser the organization's policy prohibiting retaliation. Explain that the person may be held accountable for any behavior that is construed as retaliation against the complainant.

5. *Communicate to the complainant the results of the meeting with the alleged harasser. This may be by phone or in person, depending on the request of the complainant.* Remember, you must get back to the complainant as soon as possible with the details of the meeting. Explain how it went and what you and the alleged harasser discussed. Explain any major discrepancies in the two views of the situation. Note any changes in the complainant's story at this time. Let the complainant know what the alleged harasser agreed to do. If the person denied that anything happened, inform the complainant of this.

The complainant may wish to go forward with a formal charge if she or he feels that the alleged harasser does not intend to change his or her behavior. Remain available to assist the complainant in the future if there are more questions. Depending on how the meeting with the alleged harasser went, it is possible that future meetings may be needed to get the offensive behavior(s) to stop.

Handling a sexual harassment complaint is never easy. Even under the best of all possible circumstances, the conversations are often awkward, uncomfortable, and frequently very emotionally charged. However, an informal resolution process that utilizes the preceding suggestions can help both the complainant and the alleged harasser feel as though they were heard and understood in a timely, confidential, and professional manner.

HOW TO MANAGE YOUR CAREER EFFECTIVELY

Gerald Sturman

Gerald Sturman, *Ph.D., is chairman and CEO of The Career Development Team (19 Brookwood Road, Bedford, NY 10506, 914-234-3200, js@world..std.com, http//world. std.com/njs), a national consulting firm in organizational career management. He is the author of* **If You Knew Who You Were … You Could Be Who You Are!** *(Bierman House, Inc.),* **Coaching Careers and Performance,** *and the chapter on "Career Development and Growth" in the* **AMA Handbook for Developing Employee Assistance & Counseling Programs.**

This guide provides a step-by-step approach to managing your career effectively to achieve personal success and satisfaction. It is chock full of information about every aspect of the career management process.

The career management process has five major components that spell out the leading letters of the words "aim at career management": AIM…CM. The five components are *assessment, investigation, matching, choosing,* and *managing.* The broad meanings of these processes are given in Figure 37.1.

Assessment

The career management process starts with learning as much as possible about yourself in relation to your worklife. Four elements define who you are in relation to your worklife:

1. *Your style:* How you do what you do.
2. *Your motivation:* Why you do what you do.
3. *Your skills:* What you use to do what you do.
4. *Your internal barriers:* What blocks you from doing what you do as well as you can.

A Assess your style, skills, personal qualities, interests, barriers, developmental needs, vision of your worklife, and other factors required to provide a clear understanding of yourself in relation to your worklife.

I Investigate the environment around you and discover the opportunities: first, in your current job, then in your department and division and company; then in the economy and in other organizations and industries. What is present now and what changes will the future bring?

M Match your assessment of yourself with the opportunities. Where can you make the greatest contribution consistent with your own vision and the needs and challenges of the environment?

C Choose development targets.

M Manage your career with power!

Plan your development: specific goals and targets, action steps, schedules, barriers to be overcome, required resources, and support.

Obtain input from others. Get feedback from peers, manager, family, objective third parties (human resource professionals, counselors, mentor, colleagues, and the like).

Work it! Take action with energy, intention, and know-how. Handle the barriers and express your commitment.

Evaluate results. Measure results against goals.

Revise your plan as needed and keep working it.

Figure 37.1. The Career Management Process.

You can think about these elements on your own, but you should also consider using published self-assessments. Here are some to consider:

Style: Two elements of style should be examined: *psychological type* and *career type*. A good way to determine your psychological type (or temperament) is from the book *Please Understand Me, Character and*

Temperament Types, by David Keirsey and Marilyn Bates, distributed by Prometheus Nemesis Book Company, PO Box 2748, Del Mar, CA 92014. This book contains an assessment tool that leads to a determination of 16 psychological types. Detailed descriptions of the 16 types are given, and information on style is included with information on career and job preferences and work style. Career type has to do with the relationship of your personality to the kinds of work that you like to do, the occupations you choose, and the work environments in which you thrive. A simple approach to determine your career style is the *Self-Directed Search (SDS),* available from Psychological Assessment Resources, Inc. (PAR), PO Box 98, Odessa, FL 33556, 813-968-3003.

Motivation: The three most important elements of motivation are your *career interests,* your *career anchors,* and your *career values and needs.*

Career interests may be determined from the *Self-Directed Search,* mentioned previously. The most widely used career interest assessment is the *Strong Interest Inventory.* It is available from The Psychological Corporation, Harcourt Brace Jovanovich, Inc., 555 Academic Court, San Antonio, TX 78204-2498, 800-228-0752.

Your career anchor is your self-image of what you excel in, want, and value. It provides reasons for the choices that you make because you are likely to try to fulfill your own self-image. The *Career Anchors* inventory and information about this assessment are available from Pfeiffer & Company, 2780 Circleport Drive, Erlanger, KY 41018, 800-274-4434.

Career values and needs describe the dimensions of your work that you regard as important sources of satisfaction or that represent pressing and essential elements of your life and work. A good tool for determining values and needs is the *Values Card Sort.* This tool is available from Career Research and Testing, 2005 Hamilton Avenue, Suite 250, San Jose CA 95125, 408-559-4945.

Skills: Skills may be divided into three categories: functional skills, adaptive skills, and specific content skills. *Functional skills* are the skills that we use to deal with people, data, or things. Examples include organizing information logically, communicating clearly, writing with style, lifting heavy objects, analyzing and solving problems, making decisions, and relating effectively to people. *Adaptive skills* (sometimes called self-management skills or personal qualities and characteristics) are those qualities that you learn because you need or choose to use them to fit yourself into specific environments, for example, home, school, friends, and work. Examples include punctuality, self-organization, patience, and tact. *Specific content skills* are the ones used only in a particular job. Examples include knowing how to operate a specific mainframe computer or a tower crane, performing open-heart surgery, assembling microcircuit boards, knowledge of tax law and how to make out a tax return, knowledge of a specific computer language, and how to grow orchids.

Skills may be assessed using the *Skills Card Sort,* also available from Career Research and Testing. Large inventories of skills may be found throughout the career development literature. For example, in Richard Bolles best-selling book *What Color Is Your Parachute?* published by Ten Speed Press.

Internal Barriers and Developmental Needs: These critical factors in assessment are best determined through the use of the comprehensive inventories also available in *What Color Is Your Parachute?* A comprehensive set of style, motivation, skills, and barriers inventories is available in the author's book *If You Knew Who You Were ... You Could Be Who You Are!,* published by Bierman House, Inc., 19 Brookwood Road, Bedford, NY 10506, 914-234-3200.

Investigation

Effective career management requires being awake to your career environment and aware of what is going on in the world that affects your career, now and in the future. Your career environment is much larger than your present job or company and includes elements all the way out to the world economy (see Figure 37.2).

Reading for Career Information: The nest of circles in Figure 37.2 defines your career environment. In each circle, there are materials you need to read to keep current. For example, materials on your department and division include memos, the company newsletter, notes from departmental or division meetings, and divisional product or service announcements. Information on your company includes newsletters; product or service announcements; and newspaper, magazine, and journal articles about people, products, finances, and other information on your company. As you reach out into your industry, information on your competitors becomes important. Again, newspaper, magazine, and journal articles are useful, along with any product or service information published by your competitors. The national and world economy is best researched through newspapers, magazines, and journals.

Figure 37.2. Your career environment.

Look at everything you read from the point of view of these questions:

✓ How can this information directly or indirectly affect my job, my department, my division, or my company, and is there any action that I can take to use the information in a productive way?

✓ How does this information relate to my long-term goals?

✓ Who can I share this information with who might not have seen it but could put it to good use—my colleagues, my boss, my VP, my CEO?

The best of the national newspapers, magazines, and journals that should be read periodically include *The Wall Street Journal, The New York Times, Barron's, Forbes, Fortune, Business Week, Financial Times,* and the *Harvard Business Review.* Also useful are magazines such as *Inc.,* which contains news and information about small companies and entrepreneurial business that may have an important effect on the future of your own company and career. It is also important to look at specific industry trade magazines and professional journals associated with your career field.

Career Networking: Networking is the art and science of establishing relationships and maintaining communication with people that are useful to you and to whom you can be useful. Everyone you know can be part of your network—friends, colleagues, bosses, personal and professional acquaintances, relatives, fellow commuters, the person next to you on an airplane, hired consultants, former classmates, and reaching beyond each of these people to their own networks.

Your career network has two major purposes:

1. You want to know as many people as possible in order to be able to make a wide range of requests.

2. You want as many people as possible to know you so that they will make requests of you.

Here are some of the questions you should be asking:

✓ What principal challenges is the organization currently facing?

✓ What were the key problems in the recent past and how were they handled?

✓ What do you see as the greatest changes that might occur in the next few years? New technologies? Leadership changes? Market changes? Changes in competition? Change in the importance to the company of the work produced by the department?

✓ What is the most important thing contributed by the work done here to the company as a whole?

- ✓ What critical skills will be needed in the organization in the next few years?
- ✓ What personal qualities do you usually look for when bringing a new person into the group?
- ✓ What is the boss's principal management style? Strengths and weaknesses? Does he or she develop people? Promote them? Challenge them? Allow risk taking? Encourage taking responsibility? Who is the principal decision maker?
- ✓ With which other organizations do you usually have the most communication?
- ✓ What positions might be opening up in the future? What will be the specific requirements for skills, qualities, experience?

Matching

The next step in the process is creating a match between what you learned about yourself in the assessment phase and what you learned about the environment in the investigation phase. For each job, career, or work situation that you might consider, ask the following questions:

1. Will my preferred style fit the work situation and will I be satisfied working in the way that the job requires?
2. Are the specific activities in the job things that I like to do and can either do well or learn to do well?
3. Do the kinds of people with whom I will work match my style and ways of doing things, or are they tolerant and supportive of differences in style?
4. How do my style and my future boss's style compare? Are they compatible?
5. Is the physical environment in which I would work one that would be satisfying for me?
6. Is the organizational culture suited to my temperament and values?
7. Do I have any barriers that would get in my way in the environment?
8. Is the specific contribution I would be making one that appeals to me?
9. Is the opportunity for my personal growth and development suitable to my needs?
10. Is the compensation appropriate to the contribution that I will make and to my financial needs?

Answering these questions will allow you to make more appropriate choices of jobs, positions, career directions, and promotional opportunities and to make clearer decisions about where you should be working.

Once you have discovered your best opportunity, you will probably need to choose development targets so that you can perform as well as possible. This is true even if you plan to stay in your current job.

If you have answered all the questions in the previous matching phase, you will be able to consider what kind of development you might need for either your current position or for a new job or career. In particular, answers to question 2 relating to the specific activities that you will have to do on the job will point to specific forms of skills development.

Development activities include reading books, watching videotapes, listening to audiotapes, computer-assisted learning, training courses, degree programs, on-the-job training, information networking, and others. A good exercise for discovering development activities is to brainstorm with a group of friends or colleagues about a particular need that you have. It may also be useful to sit down with your boss and discuss your developmental needs in light of what you discovered in your assessment. Remain open to his or her suggestions. There is always both the need and the opportunity for personal and professional development. Make it a lifelong activity.

Finally, you are ready to begin managing your career with p–o–w–e–r. There are five steps in career management. To make them simple to remember, we have given them the acronym p–o–w–e–r, which stands for Plan, Obtain feedback, Work it, Evaluate the results, and Revise the plan.

(P) Plan Your Development

A good plan includes the following elements:

✓ A statement of purpose
✓ Specific goals to be reached
✓ Action steps required to reach the goals
✓ Schedule of implementation
✓ Barriers that can be expected to block progress
✓ Resources required for implementation and when they will be required

Purpose statement: Your statement of purpose should clearly state what you are going to do and why you are going to do it. A typical purpose statement for a career plan might be the following: "The purpose of this plan is to provide a clear guide for my activities over the next three years so that I can be working in my new position by the end of that period." If you are planning to stay in your current position, your career plan purpose statement might state that "The purpose of this plan is to create a list of activities and a schedule for my personal development so that I can expand my ability to excel in my current position."

Specific goals: While the purpose statement provides an overall intended result to be achieved, your goals represent specific achievements along the way. An effectively stated goal has three characteristics: (1) It is clear and specific, (2) it is measurable, and (3) you have a reasonable chance of reaching it.

Action steps: A plan is implemented by taking the actions required to achieve the goals. The action required should be broken down into distinct steps, a small number of substeps that can be accomplished in a reasonable time. For example, if a specific goal is to earn an M.B.A., a major action step might be to go to graduate school. Using this statement as an action step, however, is not an effective way to plan because going to graduate school requires too many substeps that should be spelled out in detail. A goal along the way might be to receive admission to one of the top business schools in the country. The action steps toward this goal might include (1) write to Harvard, Stanford, Northwestern, Sloan, Wharton, and Columbia, and request applications; (2) fill out applications and mail them back; (3) call network contacts for each school and promote letters of recommendation; (4) schedule interviews at each school; and so on. Note that the action steps are discrete and doable and that you can tell when each is done and how it moves you closer to the goal.

Schedule of implementation: The schedule should include the following dates:

✓ The date by which each goal will be achieved.

✓ The date by which each action step will be completed.

✓ The date by which each resource is required to be on hand.

When scheduling your plan, remember the following rules:

✓ Everything takes longer than you think it will.

✓ If something can go wrong that will extend the time required to complete something, assume that it will.

✓ Other people have their own schedules.

✓ Priorities change all the time—yours and everyone else's.

✓ Heroes die on the battlefield.

✓ Life is a process in which your vision unfolds before your eyes if you keep your eyes open and focus on the vision.

Expected barriers: It is important that you prepare yourself for the barriers that will come along as you implement your development plan. If you are prepared by knowing which barriers are most likely to emerge and have a clear sense about what can be done about them when they do hit, you have a good chance of getting through them and proceeding with your plan.

One good way to handle expected barriers is to share your expectations with others and ask for their support. Using the example of sending letters to graduate schools of business, let others know that the best thing that they can do to support you is to be unflagging in their efforts to push you to get the letters out.

Summing resources: If you include in your plan who and what you need and when you need them, you have a much better chance of having those resources available at the right time. If you go to your boss two days before you leave for another department, you may find yourself up against a barrier you cannot get through. If your boss has been a party to your plan for the past year, he or she may be prepared for your leaving and supportive of your goals. If you need to borrow money for graduate school or apply to your organization for external training funds, remember that raising money always takes time. It is valuable to know exactly how much you will need and when you will need it.

(O) Obtain Feedback

The next step in the p–o–w–e–r cycle is to obtain feedback on your plan. The purpose of this feedback is to test the reality of your plan, to have others look at it from their point of view as to what will work and not work, to gather suggestions about improving the plan and making it as workable as possible, and to enlist others in supporting you in implementing the plan. Feedback should be obtained from the following kinds of people:

1. People whose opinion about career matters you trust
2. People to whom it would be politically wise to show your plan
3. People who would be willing to support you in implementing your plan
4. People who you need to support you in implementing your plan
5. People who might benefit from your plan

The most important people are your boss and your spouse or partner. Your development plan will have a significant effect on both, and they need to know what you have in mind. If you feel that it would be impolitic, difficult, troublesome, uncomfortable, inappropriate, or otherwise not a good idea to get feedback on your plan from either your boss, your spouse or partner, or both, your plan probably expresses some significant changes in your worklife and should be thought through very carefully.

Other people with whom it is important to share your plan include anyone who may be serving as your mentor; people in your network who may have important insights into one or more of your goals (executives, economists, journalists, technical experts, and others knowledgeable in the world of modern business); people who have successfully been down the road you plan to travel; colleagues or people from other organizations who are on similar career paths; and a professional career counselor.

(W) Work It!

Use your development plan, particularly the action steps and the schedule, as a guide to your progress. Integrate your plan with the rest of your work. When you prepare your schedule for the day, look over your plan. Your daily to-do list, or whatever personal management system you use, should contain any elements of your action steps that need to be implemented.

(E) Evaluate Results

If you have written and followed your plan carefully, evaluating the results is easy. In particular, you will compare the specific goals and schedule that you have established with the goals that you have reached and when you reached them. It is also valuable to look at those goals that have not been achieved on schedule and discover what specific barriers blocked your success.

(R) Revise Your Plan

This is your own personal development plan. Feel absolutely free to revise it as often and as radically as necessary. Situations will change quickly and dramatically. The only mistake is to give up planning and working at it or to keep on going down a path that is not leading anywhere. The true career entrepreneur stays in the game and keeps on changing goals, action steps, and schedules until results are achieved.

Go for it!

HOW TO VALIDATE WHAT PEOPLE DO ON THE JOB

James Sullivan

Jim Sullivan, *Ed.D., offers workshops for trainers to certify performance of critical skills in industry. He is professor of workforce education and development at Southern Illinois University, Carbondale, IL (618-453-3321). Jim's works include standardized tests for mechanics and technicians and several technical texts. He trained as a mechanic in the hills of West Virginia and now lives on a farm in Southern Illinois where he raises hay for the horse market.*

How do you make certain that a training course teaches the "right" skills or that certification tests measure what actually needs to be achieved back on the job? The answer is by validating a task inventory. The following guide details the basic steps and procedures necessary for you to validate such an inventory for your next training course.

A valid task inventory lists what incumbents do on the job. It is the basis for identifying the skills, knowledge, and attitudes from which training courses and certification tests are developed. *Valid* means that the task inventory has been subjected to referendum by incumbents, who agree that these are the tasks that make up the job. No one knows better than incumbents what tasks make up the work that they do.

You can build and validate task inventories in a number of ways:

1. Use the DACUM method (Norton, 1985) to build a task list with a group of incumbents and their supervisors. Basically, this is an interview technique that identifies tasks at the work site. Thereafter, the task inventory is subjected to third-party validation by surveying incumbents, advisory committee members, or constituents designated by the agency contracting for the work. Special training to become a DACUM facilitator is available. Most occupational tests are developed from a task inventory generated by some variation of the DACUM process (Whitener, 1993).

2. Assemble a task inventory from a number of sources such as vocational–technical and regional curriculum centers (MAVCC, 1994) (ISCC, 1994) (CPC, 1994) and then validate it by surveying incumbents and their supervisors.

3. Use some combination of assembled task inventory and incumbent worker interviews to validate the task inventory.

You validate a task inventory to be sure you have the "right stuff" from which to build a training course or certification test. If you don't have the right tasks to start with, it is unlikely that your course will teach the right skills or that your test will measure achievement of important outcomes. From a legal standpoint, retain validation records as convincing evidence that your training courses and certification tests have content validity.

Procedure

Basically, the validation process uses rating scales to quantify a qualitative measure. Moreover, validity is measured indirectly using criteria such as importance, frequency, and difficulty. Also, remember that validity is site-specific. For example, the DACUM method may generate valid tasks at the company where interviews were conducted, but you cannot assume that the same tasks will be valid within the same company at different sites or in companies with similar job titles at various locations. Thus, if your task inventory is to be used to structure a training course or certification test for the same job across various industries and locations, validation of an assembled task inventory at representative work sites will likely produce more valid results. Figure 38.1 lists four common criteria for validating task inventories and their definitions.

Before you rate each task for importance, frequency, or difficulty, it is necessary to know if incumbents actually perform the task. If an incumbent does not perform the task, he or she cannot rate it. For the same reason, trainers, who are invaluable in developing courses, are excluded from validating tasks, because the results generated typ-

---

1. *Occurrence:* lets you know how many incumbents perform the task. Before rating a task, the incumbent must indicate that he or she has actually performed the task.

2. *Importance:* measures the degree to which an incumbent needs to be able to perform the task to be successful at the job.

3. *Frequency:* measures how often the task is performed on a daily, weekly, monthly, or annual basis. Raters decide which time frames are most appropriate.

4. *Difficulty:* measures how much training, experience, ability, and effort are required to perform or learn the task.

Figure 38.1. Task-rating Criteria.

ically do not agree with those of the incumbents who actually perform the job. Moreover, experience validating task inventories and test items with mechanics and their trainers has shown the activity to be less efficient timewise, sometimes taking twice as long to perform with trainers.

Final Selection of Tasks

Incumbents who indicate that they have performed a given task establish how it rates relative to other tasks in the inventory and whether to keep or discard the task as the basis for constructing a course or building a certification test. A common estimate for the cutoff line in a task inventory is arrived at by using the 75% rule, which excludes tasks that are not performed by at least 75% of incumbents. Thus only tasks that are performed by 75% or more of incumbents are used to construct courses or build certification tests. Of course, the final decision about which tasks to keep and which to discard is made by an advisory committee representing the organization accepting the work, but it is helpful for you to recommend an estimate to focus discussions about where to draw the line. And while advisory committees typically accept tasks that are performed by more than 75% of incumbents for inclusion, it is not uncommon to have them lower the standard to include some tasks performed by fewer incumbents for various reasons, including safety and infusing new technology into the job.

How to Establish Instructional Order

Use measures of validity, such as importance, frequency, and difficulty, separately to make decisions about what to teach. For example, if a task does not achieve a certain importance or frequency rating, it could be deleted from a final task inventory altogether.

Sometimes you will combine measures of validity to make decisions about when a particular task will be taught in an instructional program. For example, equation 38.1 combines three criteria to make a decision about the ordering of instructions to teach specific tasks:

$$IO = I + (F - D) \qquad (38.1)$$

where IO is the instructional order in which a task will be taught, I is the importance rating, F is the frequency rating, and D is the difficulty rating. Notice that the formula assigns frequency and difficulty opposite effects on instructional order. That is, the formula favors teaching tasks first that are important and performed more frequently than those that, while still important, are performed less frequently and are more difficult to perform and learn.

In general, there is a positive correlation between ratings for occurrence and calculated values for instructional order. That is, if a task is performed by a high percentage of incumbents who validate a task inventory across several work sites, it also is likely to generate higher computed values for instructional order. Remember that task occurrence rates tasks by the percentage of incumbents who actually perform the task, while instructional order combines the importance, frequency, and difficulty of each task to establish which tasks will be taught first in a training course. The instructional order formula will reorder tasks that are rated for occurrence by the same percentage of incumbents. And, more significant, if the task is completed by all incumbents, you must still establish where various tasks will be placed in the instructional sequence.

Role of the Facilitator

The role of the facilitator in validating a task inventory is to identify incumbents who actually perform the task, meet them at the work site, make them feel comfortable, conduct a joint interview in which they can interact, and have each incumbent complete a separate task inventory instrument. After 10 to 15 minutes of introductions, during which time you explain the purpose for the interview and build personal credibility, have each incumbent complete an information form that asks for demographic and job-related information. You need this to document your work and associate ratings with specific incumbents and their jobs. Then start with the first task and work through the occurrence, importance, frequency, and difficulty ratings criteria. During this time, encourage discussion, but have each incumbent record individual ratings for the tasks using a separate task inventory instrument to reflect his or her job experience. Now ask one incumbent what he or she thinks about the next task, essentially designating a discussion leader for that task. Establish a pattern by having another incumbent discuss the next task, and so on, so that you can assume the role of a listener, while incumbents take turns discussing tasks in sequence. If new tasks come out of the discussion, jot those down and have them rated as well.

Identifying incumbents who actually perform the tasks may sound like a contradiction, but often people who perform the work in question are indispensable at the work site, and a supervisor or trainer who does not actually perform the tasks will be assigned to the interview instead. Try to head this off by establishing ground rules to select incumbents when the interviews are being arranged, but if this occurs there is no graceful way to cancel the interview. Instead, complete the interview, but keep these data separate. It is useful to contrast supervisory and instructional personnel ratings with incumbent ratings, but they will be enough different to justify not combining them. You also will notice that in a mixed group trainers feel intimidated in the presence of incumbents rating tasks that are not performed as part of the trainer's responsibilities. That is, the rating is made up from imagined or sympathetic participation in the activity or from past experience, rather than from current experience as an incumbent. Try to avoid this situation if possible.

Definitions and rating scales used by incumbents for criteria are given in Figure 38.2. They can be modified to suit a particular job. The rating form used by incumbents to record their judgments is given in Figure 38.3.

Item 1: Task Occurrence

Have you ever performed this task in your job? (Tasks not included in the inventory should be written in the available space and checked.) Rate each task as either **yes** or **no**.

Item 2: Task Importance to the Job

How important is this task to performing your job? That is, do you have to perform this task to perform your job? Rate each task as follows:

1. Unimportant
2. Moderately important
3. Important
4. Very important
5. Highly important

Item 3: Frequency of Performance

How often do you perform this task in your job? Rate each task as follows:

1. Once a year
2. Once every 6 months
3. Once a month
4. Once a week
5. One or more times each day

Item 4: Task Difficulty

How difficult is it to perform or learn each task that you do? Rate each task as follows:

1. *Easy:* This could be done by an entry-level person.
2. *Moderate difficulty:* An apprentice or person with training could complete the task.
3. *Difficult:* Journeyman skills or training and some experience are required to perform the task.
4. *Very difficult:* Journeyman with specialized skills and training is required.
5. *Extremely difficult:* Master with skills, training, and extensive experience is required to perform the task.

Figure 38.2. Task Inventory Rating.

Tasks:	Occurrence Yes	No	Importance Rating	Frequency Rating	Difficulty Rating	Instructional Order
_____	___	___	[1][2][3][4][5]	[1][2][3][4][5]	[1][2][3][4][5]	___
_____	___	___	[1][2][3][4][5]	[1][2][3][4][5]	[1][2][3][4][5]	___
_____	___	___	[1][2][3][4][5]	[1][2][3][4][5]	[1][2][3][4][5]	___
_____	___	___	[1][2][3][4][5]	[1][2][3][4][5]	[1][2][3][4][5]	___
_____	___	___	[1][2][3][4][5]	[1][2][3][4][5]	[1][2][3][4][5]	___
_____	___	___	[1][2][3][4][5]	[1][2][3][4][5]	[1][2][3][4][5]	___
_____	___	___	[1][2][3][4][5]	[1][2][3][4][5]	[1][2][3][4][5]	___
_____	___	___	[1][2][3][4][5]	[1][2][3][4][5]	[1][2][3][4][5]	___
_____	___	___	[1][2][3][4][5]	[1][2][3][4][5]	[1][2][3][4][5]	___
_____	___	___	[1][2][3][4][5]	[1][2][3][4][5]	[1][2][3][4][5]	___
_____	___	___	[1][2][3][4][5]	[1][2][3][4][5]	[1][2][3][4][5]	___
_____	___	___	[1][2][3][4][5]	[1][2][3][4][5]	[1][2][3][4][5]	___
_____	___	___	[1][2][3][4][5]	[1][2][3][4][5]	[1][2][3][4][5]	___
_____	___	___	[1][2][3][4][5]	[1][2][3][4][5]	[1][2][3][4][5]	___

Figure 38.3. Task Inventory Rating Form.

223

To aggregate the data, start by summing responses for occurrence, task by task, and divide each sum by the total number of incumbents and multiply by 100. For example, if 11 of 22 incumbents interviewed performed task 1, then $11/22 \times 100 = 50\%$ of incumbents perform the task. When this calculation has been performed for each task, reorder the task list from highest to lowest percentage.

Now compute the average rating for importance, frequency, and difficulty for each task. To do this, use a blank survey form to sum the number of ratings for each task under the 5, 4, 3, 2, 1 ratings like that shown in Figure 38.4 for 11 incumbents. Then multiply the sum of the ratings by the weighted value of each rating and add them together. The example in Figure 38.4 shows the multiplication of weighted values and their sums divided by 11 incumbents to arrive at an average value of 3.18 for task importance.

Importance

(1) (2) (3) (4) (5)

1 1 4 5 0

Importance average = $(1 \times 1) + (1 \times 2) + (4 \times 3) + (5 \times 4) + (0 \times 5) = 35/11 = 3.18$

Figure 38.4. Calculating Task Values.

With average rated values computed for importance, frequency, and difficulty, compute the instructional order using equation 38.1. For example, if a task has an average rating of 3 for importance, 5 for frequency, and 2 for difficulty, the instructional order (IO) score would be:

$$IO = I + (F - D)$$
$$IO = 3 + (5 - 2) = 6$$

Theoretically, numbers for instructional order range from a high of 9 to less than 0, although it is more common to see a range from 9 to 3. Tasks with ratings less than 3 are typically not very important, not frequently performed, but difficult to perform, and often do not make the 75% rule for acceptance.

The finished task list includes job titles and incumbent profiles for which the task inventory has application. It also contains the cutoff point. First, assemble the validated task inventory in hierarchical order with the cutoff line drawn below the last task that is performed by 75% of incumbents. To document the task list, also assemble a listing of incumbents who were interviewed and their job titles and definitions, interview dates, and contact person at the site. If the task inventory will be used to construct a certification exam, this may be sufficient to begin building the test.

Finally, if you are to develop an instructional program, record average ratings for importance, frequency, and difficulty for each task to evaluate the relative value of each criterion and to establish instructional order using equation 38.1.

REFERENCES

CPC. 1994. McComb, IL: Curriculum Publications Clearinghouse. Western Illinois University.

Hattaway, Brenda, and Ron McCage. 1993. "V-tecs direct: a resource for the 90's." Indianapolis, IN: The fourth national conference on competency-based assessment and performance standards for vocational–technical education. April, pp. 28–38.

ISCC. 1994. Springfield, IL: Illinois State Curriculum Center. Sangamon State University.

MAVCC. 1994. Stillwater, OK: Mid-america Vocational Curriculum Consortium.

Norton, Robert E. 1985. *Dacum Handbook.* Columbus, OH: Center on Education and Training for Employment (CETE).

Whitener, Scott. 1993. *The National Occupational Competency Testing Institute* (uses what is known as Turbo DACUM, which is a team-based, computer-assisted system to validate tasks at the work site). Big Rapids, MI: Ferris State University.

HOW TO MAKE S.U.R.E. YOUR TRAINING IS EFFECTIVE

Rick Rogers

Rick H. Rogers *is manager of compliance training for Astra USA, Inc. (50 Otis Street, Westborough, MA 01581, 508-366-1100), a manufacturer of ethical pharmaceuticals, as well as a professor of management at Bentley College. Rick is also a past president of the Bio-Pharmaceutical Education and Training Association and chairs the PDA's interest group on training.*

This guide quickly reviews two common course design errors and then presents a four-step model that helps you to avoid these problems in your own training programs.

Have you ever found yourself worried that participants in your training were not getting very much out of the session? It's really tough when your participants sit through a whole class and then walk out saying "I didn't get anything out of that, did you?" Are your participants saying these kind of things about *your* sessions?

Two Common Errors

Training designers experience two very common, yet avoidable, errors. These problems contribute to a session being less effective than it should be, thus wasting time, money, and effort on training activities that do not give either the participants or the organization the payback that they deserve.

1. *Lack of ownership.* The first common error occurs when the design provides no way for the participants to "own" the training activity, to be really vested in what they are doing. Ownership of the session is vital to adult learners. If the participants do not have a reason for why they should be in your session, then you cannot expect to achieve all your training objectives.

   Example: *A very common example is the training session that only attempts to convey information (the boring lecture). No effort is made to*

226

*link the session to something of value to the participants. This lack of ownership in the design forces the participants to try to **devise for themselves** a potential use or application for the information. Wouldn't your session be a lot more effective if the design **facilitated** the participants' need to form an application for the topic?*

2. *Lack of involvement in the content.* Being involved in the content is far different from merely being involved in the session. Staying involved in the classroom session itself is indeed important and adds to the overall learning experience. However, the participants' learning experience and the overall effectiveness of the session can fail badly if the participants are not truly involved in the content, as well as the context, of the session. The participants' interest in and use of the session objectives are the primary reasons for the session. The training design that does not take this into account generally cannot make good use of the session time.

    Example: *Recall a session you've attended that was very enjoyable but that did not accomplish much. The participants had a good time, but they did not learn anything of value.*

Four Keys

Now think back to your own training courses. Can you say that your participants came away from your sessions with a plan in hand for actually doing something different back on the job? Did you feel that your participants really got involved in the material? Or were they just going through the motions? If you are not sure about the answers to these questions, then it is possible that these two common errors are sneaking in to your designs. That's the bad news.

The good news is that these errors are not difficult to fix, and once you have made the appropriate changes, you will have four tools that can greatly enhance your effectiveness as a training designer. The two common errors described above can easily be mitigated by applying four simple keys to the design of all your training sessions, regardless of the medium. These four keys will unlock the power of the adult learner in your sessions. Use these keys to make **S.U.R.E.** that your training is accomplishing everything you want from your design efforts. These keys are summarized in Figure 39.1.

1. *Start at the end.* Ask yourself, "What is it that I want the participants to do with the session once it is over?" How do you want them to apply the materials that you have just presented? There has to have been a need that you were trying to meet when you designed the session in the first place and some change in behavior for which you are hoping.

    Build the answer to this question into the initial icebreaker exercise, right up front. Provide the participants with a way to come to an awareness and a sense of ownership of the session. Your objective

Make S.U.R.E. of your training.

S. START with the ending.

U. UNDERSCORE the message personally.

R. REFOCUS, constantly, on the payback.

E. ENGAGE the participants with questions.

Figure 39.1.

is to have the participants thinking something like "Wow! If I get something out of this session (video, CBT, and so on) today I'll be able to do X!" Of course, X is your behavioral objective for the session, the hoped for behavior change back on the job.

    Example *(for a time management course): Add a short questionnaire to the icebreaker. Part of the questionnaire would typically ask for the name, position, how long with the organization, and the like. One last question, though, could be something like "Name two things that keep you from doing what you want to get done." Have the group introduce themselves via the questionnaire, and as they do so, flip chart the answers to the last question. Your flip chart will be a list of time wasters that the participants can use to formulate a concrete list of potential payoffs. Post this list prominently for reference throughout the session. It can be used to touch the participants personally, which leads us to the second key to effective design.*

2. *Underscore the message personally.* Focus the participants on the potential payoffs for themselves right at the end of the original icebreaker or introductory exercise.

    Example *(the time management course again): Pause at the close of the vesting exercise, point to the flip chart, and ask the participants something like "If you had a tool that could get rid of, or even just reduce, one or more of these items, would you make more money for yourself? Would you have more time to do the things you really want to do?"*

    To answer this question, the participants will have to formulate some personal payback for themselves. The answer they come up with (have them write it down) will be in the present tense. It will be something that they want to accomplish now. It will be something of their own design. It will be concrete, and it will be of value to them personally. Most importantly, they will be involved in the content of your session because they have something in front of them, or in the front of their minds, that is of value to them personally.

Finish up this exercise by pointing out that the reason for their attendance is to attempt to answer just these questions during the session. The participants will begin to experience the session as something almost custom designed for them.

3. *Refocus on the payback constantly.* It is not enough to vest your participants in the course once, at the beginning, and hope that it sticks with them throughout the whole session, especially when the session is long or there is a lot of content. Your design must keep the personal value of the session in the minds of your participants throughout the session.

> **Example:** *Use the information from the original introductory exercise as a benchmark, or reference point, against the content for the remainder of the course. Remind the group several times as you move through the session that successful use of the content will help them to meet their own goals (point to their remarks on the flip chart again).*
>
> *There is no hard and fast schedule for how often to do this, although every half-hour or so is appropriate for longer sessions. Certainly, you will want to benchmark back to the initial exercise for each major part of the content. In doing so, remember to continually point out the personal relevance. Ask them to look at what they have written down as a potential payback. This is not hard to do if you write these questions right into your design, which leads to the last tool, engaging with questions.*

4. *Engage the participants with questions.* Perhaps the single most effective training tool is the question. No other skill in your training toolkit is as effective in getting the participants focused on your content or involved in the session. Questions can be written into the design throughout the module to keep the participants focused on the material and involved in the value of the material.

When writing your questions:

1. *Benchmark back to the introductory exercise. Ask your participants over and over again to recall what they concluded about how they could use the materials in their own jobs or lives.*

2. *Be personal. Ask them to ask of themselves (privately, not in public) what value the material has for them. How will they use it?*

3. *Focus attention on the material at hand.*

Make sure that the participants are asked to analyze their own situation in light of the content that the session covers.

If your design has kept the participants vested in the topic throughout the session, it will be easy for them to apply your training to their own situations. The participants who have found an application in their personal situation for the concepts that you have attempted to convey in the session will be not only willing but eager to transfer the learning to their situations. If your design has done a good job of maintaining involvement in the potential personal payback, the participants will be angry if they *don't* get a chance to apply the session to their personal situation.

If the individuals who complete training designed by you are truly more competent as a result of your efforts, aren't they likely to be more effective in their jobs? In their lives? Increased effectiveness translates into increased benefits and rewards, both for them and for your organization.

Make **S.U.R.E.** of your training. It reflects on you!

HOW TO DEVELOP A COMPUTER-BASED TRAINING SYSTEM IN A SMALL OR MEDIUM-SIZE ENTERPRISE

Horris Leung and Ruth Leung

Horris Leung *is a senior research fellow (Tel: +44 1203 523523; Email: esryj@csv.warwick.ac.uk), and* **Ruth Leung** *is a senior teaching fellow (Tel: +44 1203 524359; Email: leung-r@eeyore.warwick.ac.uk) at the department of engineering, University of Warwick, Coventry, CV4 7AL, England. Horris's current research interest includes the use of artificial neural networks and genetic algorithms in intelligent engineering systems and hypermedia applications in manufacturing. He worked as a system development manager for a precision machinery manufacturer in Hong Kong before joining Warwick. Ruth's research interest is in the formulation of manufacturing strategy, strategy development for SME, and multimedia-based training systems in manufacturing. She also worked in the manufacturing industry in Hong Kong and the Peoples Republic of China for several years.*

Is it feasible to have computer-based training in a small or medium-size organization? This guide describes a step-by-step approach for developing a computer training system geared to the needs of a small or medium-size company.

Many companies survive by just continuing with what they have done to be successful. Why should they think about changing? Why should they consider making improvements? The fact is that a competitive business environment, ever changing customer requirements, and emerging technologies have not allowed companies to stay still. Such trends have affected not just big companies, but have often meant life or death for many small and medium-size enterprises (SME). To compete in such volatile marketplaces, the whole organization must learn about new ideas and new approaches and be trained in new practices, procedures, tools, and techniques.

Books, journals, seminars, conferences, and specific training programs are common sources of information. Yet, by the very nature of SME, limited resources require that almost all staff spend their time on daily operations. Off-site training is too expensive an option to be considered. Books or journals are often too academic to be understood by general practitioners. In comparison to these conventional approaches to knowledge and skills acquisition, increasing the computer-based training system becomes a practical, flexible, and low-cost option in the organizational learning process. Therefore, the focus of this guide is to describe a step-by-step approach for SME management to develop a computer training system for their specific needs.

Feasibility of Computer-based Training in SME

Computer-based training (CBT) incorporates a computer as the medium with which to deliver training. The training materials are stored in a computer, which enables a user to systematically gain knowledge and skills through a series of interactive learning sequences. A user experiences frames on the computer screen containing step-by-step definitions, explanations, examples, problem-solving demonstrations, questions, and hands-on exercises related to that subject matter. Advanced computing technology provides the users with a vast amount of information presented in an interesting, colorful, graphical, and interactive manner. Apart from text, the presentation can be in the form of sound, video, graphic images, animation, simulations, and other computer applications, either singularly or in combination. The user is often able to manipulate the materials to be learned and control the learning process. This allows the user to respond both individually and actively to the training material. Some common advantages of computer-based training are summarized next.

Availability: Training is available whenever (any time of the day or night), wherever (almost anywhere at work or even at home), and to whomever (management, technicians, or operators).

Effective learning: CBT utilizes active exchanges of information between the computer and its users, often requiring a user response before proceeding through a learning module. Such give and take contributes positively to the effectiveness of the learning process.

Motivation: Training materials on CBT are presented in an attractive and interesting manner. The user often feels in control of the training process and can stop, pause, skip, or repeat either difficult sections or the whole lesson at any time. The user is motivated to learn according to his or her own needs and ability, avoiding any likely intimidation posed by critical instructors.

Flexible learning: CBT often allows great flexibility in the training program. It can cater to users with various backgrounds, requirements, or learning habits. A learner can follow the sequential steps designed by the system developer or can jump around unrestrictedly within the program.

Consistency: All users receive the same training materials and delivery methods.

Cost effectiveness: CBT is carried out locally, resulting in travel and work time savings. The high initial costs are often compensated for by almost unlimited training afterward.

Obviously, there are also several disadvantages to CBT that must be considered before committing to this medium. Some of the key disadvantages are described next.

Cost: CBT incurs high initial costs both in terms of computer hardware and software. Although commercial prices are decreasing, CBT is still very expensive for small companies to acquire.

Skills required: Special expertise is required in developing CBT, for example, computer programming, learning psychology, and information presentation. The cost of development is expensive if expertise is not available internally. Maintenance skills are also needed once the system is up and running.

Development time: Depending on the complexity, the whole development cycle can be a lengthy process.

Training environment: CBT is mainly designed for individual learning. If group training is required, CBT is not a viable option.

Computer literacy: Certain individuals, such as shopfloor operators, may not have any prior experience using a computer. Although CBT programs are generally very user-friendly and require little prior computer knowledge, computer novices may still need a great deal of persuasion to sign up for such courses.

It is important to stress that in many instances the decision to use CBT is not absolute. For example, whether the consistency aspect of CBT is better than conventional training very much depends on the company culture and specific training requirements. CBT is not intended to replace the human trainer completely, but rather to complement or supplement conventional training methods.

Steps in Developing a Computer-based Training System

There is a systematic step-by-step approach to developing the computer-based training system in SME. The approach is schematically described by the flow chart in Figure 40.1. The flow chart is basically a logical sequence of software project development simplified for the SME environment. It consists of four stages.

Stage I   Define the needs and training options.

Stage II   Identify the project team and the CBT system specification.

Stage III   Detail design and programming.

Stage IV   Implement and continuously improve.

The following sections further elaborate these four stages into 12 steps. Key considerations and decision points are outlined, and the specific decision tools used are included.

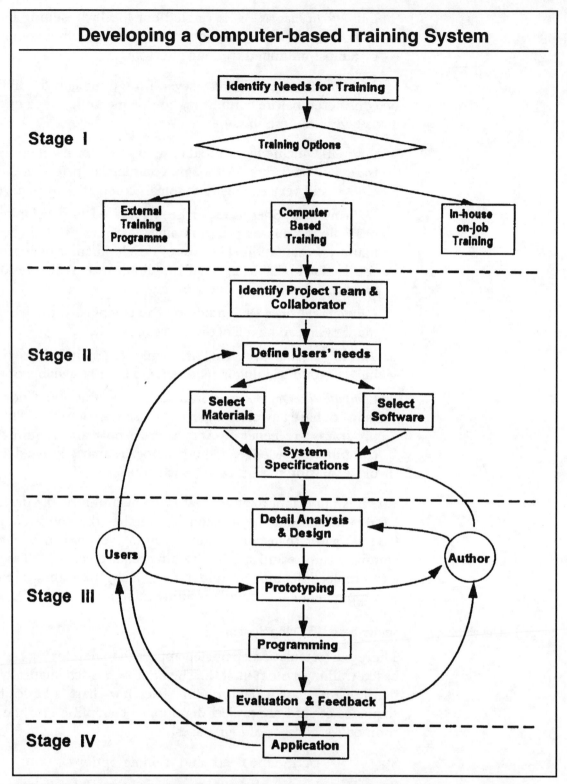

Figure 40.1. A Systematic Approach to Develop a Computer-based Training System for Small and Medium-size Enterprises.

Step 1: Identify the training needs: The first step, which is probably the most fundamental, is to assess the current training needs. Employee knowledge or skill levels in a particular subject could be at issue, or perhaps there is an overall company performance issue that needs to be addressed.

Here are some common CBT applications: the use of statistical process control (SPC) tools, formulation of basic problem-solving tools (7 QC tools), increased awareness of ISO 9000 quality standards, familiarization with operations procedures (new methods or new staff), learning of additional language and communication skills, and development of strategic management tools and techniques (quality function deployment).

The technique used to assess the current needs is identified on the *key considerations table.* To start with, the key consideration categories in regard to training are systematically listed in the left-hand column of the table. The findings of these considerations are described in the right-hand column. As an example, Table 40.1 shows a list of the possible training considerations for ISO 9000 awareness. The use of the table, apart from providing a holistic review of the training needs and guiding the decision-making process, should be treated as part of the documentation process. If there is any ambiguity in the later stage, one can always refer back to the earlier justification. This is true for the rest of the tables covered in this guide.

In a SME, this first step is likely to be the responsibility of the senior management or the training department. In other cases, individual departments can raise the issue and alert management to review the consideration table suggested in Table 40.1. It is always better to act proactively, identifying any needs before those needs actually occur; that is, plan for appropriate training before poor performance results in a lack of training.

Step 2: Evaluate the training options: The next step is to decide which training options are best for that particular circumstance and training requirements. Key training criteria are listed in the first column, similarly to step 1. Then each of these criteria is gauged against the training options or, in other words, the appropriateness of each training option against each of these criteria is established. For simplicity and visibility, we use symbols instead of numbers to represent the degree of the appropriateness. The result is then charted onto the table to give a sense of overall suitability, as shown in Table 40.2, which is an example of such decision tool. Table 40.2 is called a decision matrix. Management should be able to decide which among these training options is the best to satisfy their needs based on their prior analysis.

Table 40.1. Charting the Training Needs for Your Company.	
Fill in the appropriate description	
Considerations	*Description*
Subject/areas/skill that require training	*Awareness in ISO 9000*
Reasons for training	*Potential new customer requirements*
Audience/trainee	*Managers, engineers, planners, technicians, operators*
When training is required	*Medium to long term*
Number of employees that require training	*20 to 40*
Frequency of the training required	*3 to 4 times for the first year*
Training requirements	*Seminarts, case studies, practices*
Standard or company-specific training	*Standard and also company-specific*
Estimated duration of training	*5 to 10 days*
Who provides the training	*Quality manager*
Where training can be held	*In-house, hotels, colleges*
Funding or resources for training	*$5000*
Expected result from the training	*Acceptance of ISO 9000*
Consequences of not having the training	*Loss of existing and new customers*

Stage II: Identify the Project Team and the CBT System Specification

Step 3: Select the project team and collaborator: This stage is based on the decision that CBT is needed for the company. The first step is to form a team to carry through the project. Use a skill matrix, which is illustrated in Table 40.3, to choose team members from the resources available. The procedure here is very similar to the previous decision matrix, but for demonstration's sake, a quantified version is shown. It is as follows:

1. List the skills required to do the project in the first column of the table.

2. Identify the potential team members, and put their names down on the top.

Table 40.2. A Decision Matrix in Evaluating Training Options.

Criteria	In-house Training	External Training	Computer-based Training
Effectiveness	◉	○	●
Motivation	○	○	●
Availability	○	○	●
Flexibility	◉	⊗	●
Skills required	○	●	○
Group training	◉	●	⊗
Interactivity	◉	○	●
Initial cost	◉	●	⊗
Cost/training	○	⊗	●

Symbols for the degree of appropriateness
● most appropriate
◉ appropriate
○ least appropriate
⊗ inappropriate

3. Assess the individual's suitability against the skills required with a scale of 0 to 9, such as 0 is very poor, while 9 is the most capable. Chart them onto the table and calculate the total score.

4. If selection is just based on total scores, it can be misleading. Since these skill requirements have different degrees of significance to the project, a weight factor (0.1 to 0.9) should be included. The result from the weighted total score gives a more balanced view.

In some situations, after the skill matrix analysis, companies may conclude that they need to seek a collaborating partner to compensate for a shortage of skills. Because of the cost factor in a SME environment, collaboration can be explored with local colleges or universities, if they are agreeable to making CBT part of final-year student project requirements. Further discussion on this point will be included in the last section.

Step 4: Define the users' needs and expectations: One of the most cited company objectives is to satisfy customer needs. For such a CBT project, it is equally important to identify the user needs and satisfy them, as a company does for its customers. Either through interviews or questionnaires, a needs analysis is conducted to clarify the training objectives, scope of training, user expectations, past experience, and reactions to CBT. Apart from some specific issues, com-

Table 40. 3. Selecting Project Team Members by Using Skill Matrix Analysis.

Skill required	Weight	A	B	C	D	E
Subject knowledge	0.9	0	9	5	3	7
Programming ability	0.8	9	0	2	7	5
Information management	0.7	7	2	3	6	6
Artistic skill	0.5	3	3	5	2	6
Resourcefulness	0.3	2	6	9	5	1
Organization skill	0.4	3	5	8	7	1
Communication skill	0.6	2	5	7	6	2
Training experience	0.8	3	3	7	5	4
Analytical mind	0.6	8	4	4	6	5
Availability	0.9	8	3	3	6	8
Total score		45	40	53	53	45
Weighted total score		31.0	25.3	31.5	34.4	32.8

mon expectations could be simplicity, user-friendliness, ease of use, minimum learning requirements, high interest value, practicality, up-to-date materials, and adequate instructions. As before, these findings can be charted onto a table depicting needs for different user groups. The chart can also be used as a record for defining system specifications.

Involving users in the early stages of the development process often results in a greater chance of successful implementation.

Step 5: Select the development software: A number of CBT development or authoring tools are available on the market. It is necessary to assess their suitability for your needs. The selection criteria can include the following:

✓ *Costs:* cost of the system, cost of development, and cost of distributing the training program developed (for example, a royalty or licensing agreement)

✓ *Hardware and software platforms:* hardware compatibility and connectivity, process speed, operating system, and other software requirements

✓ *Availability and cost of technical support*

✓ *Functionality and features:* graphic interface, support of multimedia, support of interactivity between the users and the system, support of hypertext and hypermedia, simulations, and connection to other intelligent systems (for example, expert systems)

✓ *Programming expertise required*

Some popular development tools available in the markets are *Guide, Multimedia Toolbook, IconAuthor, Authorware, Knowledge Pro,* and *Hypercard.* A decision matrix analysis can be used to decide which system to purchase.

Step 6: Selection of material: One critical success factor for such a project is the content and organization of the material presented to the users. Based on step 4, the team has to define the scope of training and specific topics to be covered, identify the source and locations of information, and determine the style and presentation of the materials. After consulting with subject experts, gathering detailed information, and conducting brainstorming exercises, a meeting is held to finalize the suitability of the materials chosen.

Figure 40.2 shows an example of how the major topics of a CBT on ISO 9000 are generated by a brainstorming exercise. Each topic is then further divided into subsections.

Step 7: Define the system features and specifications: This involves translating the user requirements into specific system features and specifications. It also takes into account development tool capability. Some common specifications for a CBT are as follows:

✓ User-friendly interface

✓ Interactive use of the materials

✓ Use of multimedia presentations

✓ Annotation facility, road map, or navigation facility

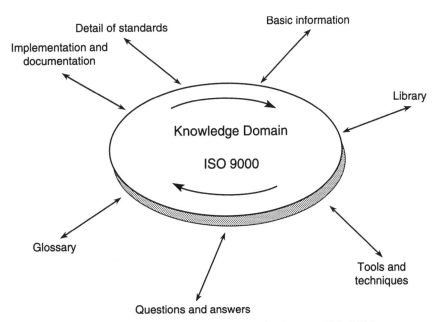

Figure 40.2. Generation of Related Contents of a CBT on ISO 9000.

✓ Help facility

✓ Hands-on exercises

✓ Assessment quiz or tests

✓ Records of training

Stage III: Detail Design and Programming

Step 8: Detail analysis and design: This step deals with the detail structuring of materials and the identification of the interrelationship between subsections. As an example, Figure 40.3 illustrates the layout and structure of a CBT. Other design issues that the project team needs to pay attention to include screen design, readability, layout, graphics, and the use of color.

Step 9: Prototyping: Instead of constructing the whole system all at once, it is wise to build a elementary prototype to eliminate any obvious structural mistakes and then test it with the potential users. After the initial test, ask the users for their opinions on the basic features and capability of the system and revise specifications if necessary before large-scale program activity.

Step 10: Programming and testing: The type of work involved in the actual programming depends very much on the chosen development tool. Some need authors with advanced programming capability, while others can be done by novices. What is important here is to test the program developed in stages, not to wait for testing until the finished product is complete.

Step 11: Evaluation: It is definitely worthwhile to carry out an evaluation of the system before actual implementation. The process is done

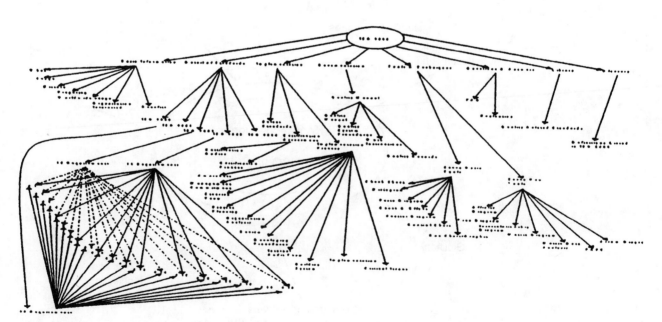

Figure 40.3. Information Structuring of a CBT.

by inviting potential users to use the system and then to validate, comment, and suggest areas of improvement. Users fill in questionnaires with regard to the system's usability, content, screen management, and overall performance. Depending on feasibility, the CBT should be refined to satisfy as much as possible the users' recommendations.

Stage IV: Implementation and Continuous Improvement

Step 12: Application: Even when the system is up and running, the project is not yet finished. Continuous improvement of the system is necessary to satisfy the users further. The performance of CBT should be compared with conventional training methods, reviewed for what has been gained and what has been lost, and updated to keep current with progressive technology. Some implementation issues are discussed next.

1. *Resources:* Often, financial resources and computer skills are two of the biggest limiting factors for developing CBT within SME. The option to collaborate with a collegiate student project is a cost-effective solution. On the one hand, many students who have the time and enthusiasm to be involved in developing computer-based training systems will lack opportunity and practical knowledge. On the other hand, companies definitely have the need to train employees, but may lack the resources to do so. As long as both parties are aware of mutual expectations, mutual benefits can be gained.

2. *Budget:* Budgeting for CBT is not as staggering as it seems to be. In terms of hardware, basically this training system requires a reasonable-performance personal computer (PC). As far as development software is concerned, the price of many authoring tools is now quite affordable. In terms of development cost, if companies have already implemented some sort of PC-based office system, such experience is largely applicable in this case. If college students are involved, development costs should be decreased.

3. *Project timing:* The project should have a set plan and milestones for each stage of system development. A rough guideline for the duration of this type of project is as follows:

    STAGE I: 1 to 2 weeks

    STAGE II: 4 to 6 weeks (depends on availability)

    STAGE III: 6 to 12 weeks (depends on complexity)

    STAGE IV: ongoing

4. *Documentation and maintenance:* Another critical success factor for the project is planned documentation. Apart from meeting minutes, which record thought processes and decision criteria, documentation of the materials used and the information structure are also vitally important. These will be used throughout the life of the CBT program for system updates and alterations.

About the Editors

Mel Silberman, Ph.D., is President of Active Training (26 Linden Lane, Princeton, New Jersey 08540, 609-924-8157, mel@tigger.jvnc.net). He is also Professor of Psychological Studies in Education at Temple University where he specializes in instructional design and team building.

He is the author of:

> *Active Training* (Lexington Books, 1990)
> *101 Ways to Make Training Active* (Pfeiffer & Co., 1995)
> *Active Learning* (Allyn & Bacon, 1996)

He is the editor of:

> *20 Active Training Programs, Vol. I* (Pfeiffer & Co., 1992)
> *20 Active Training Programs, Vol. II* (Pfeiffer & Co., 1994)

Mel has consulted for hundreds of corporate, governmental, educational, and human service organizations worldwide. His recent clients include:

AT&T International	Midlantic Bank
Merrill Lynch	Texas Instruments
Automated Data Processing	Meridian Bank
Bristol Myers-Squibb	Franklin Quest
American Insurance Group	J. P. Morgan, Inc.
Hoffman-LaRoche	U.S. Army
Bell Atlantic	Hospital of the University of PA
ARCO Chemical	Penn State University

He is also a popular speaker at professional conferences.

Carol Auerbach is an independent management consultant (609 Kingston Rd., Baltimore, MD 21212, 410-377-9257). She is a graduate of Duke University and holds an M.Ed. in Psychoeducational Processes from Temple University. A former trainer for Mellon Bank and CIGNA Corporation, she now designs and conducts training on a wide variety of topics. This is her second experience assisting Dr. Silberman; she collaborated with Mel previously on *Active Training* (Lexington Books, 1990).